MODERN CHESS OPENING TRAPS

MODERN CHESS OPENING TRAPS

by

WILLIAM LOMBARDY

INTERNATIONAL GRANDMASTER

DAVID McKAY COMPANY, INC.

New York

Modern Chess Opening Traps

First paperback edition, 1978

LIBRARY OF CONGRESS CATALOG CARD NUMBER: 70-185140

ISBN 0-679-14400-5

MANUFACTURED IN THE UNITED STATES OF AMERICA

8 9 10

DEDICATION

TO AL HOROWITZ, A DEAR FRIEND, WITHOUT
WHOSE ENCOURAGEMENT AND SUGGESTIONS THIS
WORK WOULD NOT HAVE BEEN POSSIBLE.

Preface

Modern Chess Opening Traps is by no means an exhaustive study of the openings, nor does it pretend to cover every conceivable trap within the openings. What is offered is a unique collection of trap themes that appear in modern-day practical Chess, themes that will undoubtedly reappear time and time again. Thus, unless the theme happens to be of special value as a bridge from the old to the new, that trap theme will not appear here; naturally, we do not recommend that the reader burn his old books. On the contrary, to be a complete player, he—or she—will have to consult older volumes containing those familiar sockdolagers, perhaps forgotten by many and never learned by most, which will therefore still take a devastating toll!

The 200 traps in this volume, gleaned from the very best of master Chess, will bring Chess players of every strength right up to date. All will then have another bridge to the future, as Chess marches on!

IN GRATEFUL RECOGNITION

We sincerely thank those who dauntlessly waded through the manuscript, playing over the variations and making the necessary corrections and revisions. Special recognition is due to Beth Cassidy, Emil Kalman, Billy Patterson, Steve Moffitt, Daryl Hanks, Burt Hochberg, Lorenzo Gaskill and Nat N. Snapp.

We also thank the many grandmasters and masters, the use of whose art is vital to any Chess volume and was therefore essential to *Modern Chess Opening Traps*. Since the theme of this work treats of traps variations, we could not mention specifically all those players who might have contributed to a particular line by participating either on the winning or losing side. Nevertheless, we acknowledge them all and are deeply grateful!

MODERN CHESS OPENING TRAPS

Introduction

Chess is a game of wits—perhaps the fact most responsible for scaring off skeins of would-be wood-pushers. But now, amateur, take note. Chess is also a game of halfwits, even if such a condition of mind may be only temporary. For if such players did not exist, much of the beauty of the game would necessarily be lost. If the poor *patzer*—or for that matter the experienced expert—did not frequently manage to fall into his opponent's cleverly contrived traps, no one would ever enjoy winning a game. Let's face it; we enjoy most fooling our rival.

Except for the poor unfortunate who suffers momentary Chess-blindness, thus giving away a piece simply because his opponent attacks it, there is no one who just loses. He is helped! Some schemer sits basting his adversary's fate. The lighting may be bad, the air foul, too much noise, the room too hot, too cold, and, when one is on Mount Olympus, there may be far too many over-anxious spectators hovering over the board trying to gain a glimpse of the master—all these conditions may cause the greatest discomfort; but in the end it is the brainy will spraying fine tacks over the board that causes the total collapse.

Every Chess player dreams that someday he will produce the perfect coup, the masterly stroke. Here we attempt to make that dream come true. Many of the finest traps in modern-day Chess are set forth in this volume. You will enjoy watching others fall prey to swindle after swindle, trap after trap, enjoy this so much that you will also find yourself planning similar tainted morsels with which to waylay unsuspecting future opponents. Seeing numerous examples of traditional themes in

modern settings will sharpen your skill. At last you are ready
to tackle even the most fearsome opponent.

MAXIM DESTRUCTION

A beginner soon learns the well-worn maxim *Never give up
the open file without a fight.* The position below was reached
in a seven-minute game played at the Manhattan Chess Club.
Seven-minute Chess is that variant of five-minute Chess in
which each player receives two minutes more on his clock so
as to enable him to make a greater number of gross blunders.
At five-minute Chess each player is allotted five minutes on
his clock. A player must force checkmate or his opponent's
resignation before his own time elapses, or forfeit on time.
Contrary to popular belief, many interesting and exciting
games are played at this blinding speed. Besides, it's fun!

DIAGRAM A

White, whom we—and so does he—prefer to label N.D.
(Nondescript), saw the problem and knew the proper maxim:
Open files for winners! The simple 1. RxR QxR 2. QxQ RxQ
3. N-Q2 cedes the only open file to Black. What our friend
did not, or possibly could not, calculate under such time pressure was that such a concession does not necessarily afford a
rival a won game. Unaware of the danger, White blithely
essayed the natural developing move (1. B-K3??).

Replying with blinding speed, so as not to provide his

opponent an opportunity to retract his move, Black struck his blow for originality: 1. .... Q-B3! The trap slammed shut. The threat of mate intimidates the most valiant player; so a master, well versed in Chess oratory, and checkmate techniques, has no trouble persuading instant resignation. Work it out! It's mate or the loss of the rook, clinging now quite precariously to that open file.

The saga of the open file: after 2. RxQ, RxQ checkmate; after 2. RxR, QxP checkmate. Only your own judgment, trained by practical experience, will give you the clue as to when a maxim applies.

TRAP THEMES AND PRINCIPLES

A trap in chess parlance is, quite bluntly, an ambush. A player uses any number of devices or hoaxes to deceive an unwary rival. The poor innocent is lured into the trap which shuts suddenly and decisively. There can be no escape.

A TRAP works not because one player is a dumb bunny and the other a clever fox. A TRAP succeeds because some basic principle has been violated to a greater or lesser degree. Here's a simple example. White wishes to be extra aggressive; so he plays the King's Gambit. There's another maxim: *Whenever possible, exchange flank pawns for center pawns.* Black gives White the opportunity to apply the maxim only because the case in point happens to be an exception to the rule! 1. P-K4 P-K4 2. P-KB4 N-QB3 3. *PxP*?? Q-R5+ 4. P-N3 QxKP+ and it's all over; Black wins a rook.

Clearly then, the Chess player must be thoroughly acquainted with trap themes but, more important, he must strive first to understand elementary principles and how to apply them.

The great José Raúl Capablanca, trying to help beginners in their quest for *openings* **Knowledge,** stated these principles quite succinctly. **Develop as rapidly as possible. Avoid moving any piece more than once during the course of the opening. Minor pieces, bishops and knights, should be brought out before major pieces, rooks and the queen. Make as few pawn** moves as possible, and only those moves that definitely contribute to rapid development and attack on the center.

Observing these rules, one concludes that the central element in any game is *time*. A gain or loss of a single *tempo*[1] can completely reverse the course of a game. Since time is all-important, a player will often find it advantageous to sacrifice tons of material to achieve the greater objective, usually the surrounding and checkmating of the enemy king. No wonder Capa's principles hinge on speed!

[1] From the Latin *tempus*, the term in Chess denotes loss or gain of time in terms of moves. Thus a player who gains a *tempo* gains an extra move with which to carry out his plans, or *vice versa*.

TOOLS OF THE TRAPPER

Every skilled worker has his tools. The *trapper* employs both legitimate over-the-board techniques and, just as vital to the final outcome, psychological ploys. As often as not, one plays the opponent, not the board. Knowledge of that opponent's weaknesses and development of a talent to capitalize on them make the goal of victory that much more real. Discover that one's opponent is overly subject to greed, ambition, impetuousity and one has found a rather convenient roadmap of winning Chess!

PREPARATION FOR PLAY

Whether a person plays serious tournament chess or simply for casual enjoyment, he shall always desire to be up to date. The choice of the masters is the barometer of modern openings theory and practice, which theory and practice is necessarily adopted by tournament practitioner and casual player alike. With these thoughts in mind, we have sought to include in this volume games the openings of which pertain to modern practice. Naturally, we cannot totally disregard the past; so, we do present some older material which may serve as a bridge of reference for the reader who must also consult on occasion works covering earlier periods.

4

Theory evolves and revolves. There is constant progress and also retrogression to older theoretical lines which, despite their antiquity, do offer a wealth of possibilities for analytical improvement. Without an eye to the future and the knowledge of the past, the proficiency of the amateur will be substantially reduced.

If the reader makes even a cursory examination of the openings in this volume, he should notice one outstanding fact. Opening theory, and consequently opening traps, has changed drastically. A game may end just as suddenly and brutally as in yesteryear, but, mainly owing to improved technique and advanced knowledge, combined with a plethora of published analyses found in various journals, a game stays much longer in the opening stage. True, the short sparklers continue to crop up. But frequently the opening lasts longer; so the trap may make its appearance much later. Patience!

Browse through any openings book. Flip, for instance, to the Ruy Lopez, the Sicilian or any popular debut, and then notice the exhaustive openings analyses, many variations of which run twenty or even thirty moves before a player is left to his own devices. The result is that the poorest *patzer*—and we use this term with endearment!—has not merely better moves but, in countless instances, grandmaster moves at his disposal. In other words, the "ordinary Joe" takes much longer to blunder.

The great Tarrasch once quipped, "The mistakes are all there, waiting to be made!" Chess has not changed *so* much since Tarrasch's day. The blunders come later, but they do come after all! Dear reader, you will be there to reap the benefits.

A TRAP DOES NOT FINISH THE GAME

During the depression, when a dollar was a dollar, an enthusiastic patron of the game approached noted international master and author I.A. Horowitz in the Manhattan Chess Club and challenged him to a game at the fabulous stakes of three dollars. But there was to be one condition. If the amateur

5

should be unhappy with the master's reply to a move, the amateur could pay a quarter and suggest another move, which the master would then make—mate in one notwithstanding! I.A., furtively rubbing his hands together, reluctantly accepted the deal! And so, to arms!

1. P-K4! "Why not play 1. P-Q4?" "The wily patron has something up his sleeve," thought I.A., pocketing his first quarter. And so 1. P-Q4. The game proceeded 1. ... N-KB3 2. P-QB4! "May I suggest 2. N-Q2(!)?" "Yes, of course," replied I.A., the second quarter in hand. Thus: 2. N-Q2 P-K4 3. P-K3. A third quarter changed hands, White's last move was retracted and there followed: 3. PxP N-N5 4. KN-B3. "Don't you think you ought to chase the knight instead?" cajoled our patron. "Well," reasoned I.A., "what can I lose? Even odds, I should win anyway!" With the fourth quarter tucked away, I.A., like a lamb led to the slaughter, essayed: 4. P-KR3 (?)!

After this, Black gave no quarter: 4. ... N-K6 (!). If 5. PxN Q-R5+ 6. P-N3 QxP mate! "Even a world's champion would resign here," contributed our patron, his face flushed with anticipated victory. With a touch of the master's condescendence, I.A. intoned, "You can't win by resigning!" The game continued: 5. KN-B3 NxQ 6. KxN and *White* won a long ending! After all, wasn't he the professional!

Just one word of advice. An opponent may fall into a trap, but, unless mate is administered, he won't surrender so easily. A player must be alert enough to press home the advantage on his own! Now for the traps!

1. *Alekhine Defense*

The hypermodern principle of encouraging a central pawn buildup in order to attack same from afar goes glimmering.

1. P-K4	N-KB3
2. P-K5	N-Q4
3. P-Q4	P-Q3
4. P-QB4	N-N3
5. P-B4	PxP
6. BPxP	P-QB4?

Either N-B3 or B-B4 is acceptable.

7. P-Q5!	P-K3
8. N-QB3	PxP
9. PxP	P-B5

The center may be a tempting target, but it is nevertheless quite imposing. With the text Black admits too late the error of his strategy, while he desperately clears a path for the king bishop.

10. N-B3	B-KN5
11. Q-Q4	BxN
12. PxB	B-N5
13. BxP!	0-0

Presumably Black is ready for counter-attack, having nicely completed his development at the mere, but excessive, cost of a pawn.

14. R-KN1	Q-B2

A threat easily ignored.

15. P-K6	P-B3
16. B-R6!	QxB??

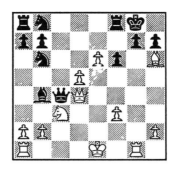

Meager resistence is offered by P-N3 giving up the exchange.

| 17. RxP+! | K-R1 |
| 18. R-N8+!! | KxR |

After . . . RxR, 19. QxP+ ends it.

| 19. Q-N1+ | K-R1 |
| 20. Q-N7 | |

Instead of the ox (the loss of a rook for a minor piece), the king is lost.

2. Alekhine's Defense

Black hesitates to accept the gambit pawn and meets the same fate he was hoping to avoid by the refusal of the sacrifice.

1. P-K4	N-KB3
2. P-K5	N-Q4
3. P-Q4	P-Q3
4. P-QB4	N-N3
5. P-B4	PxP
6. BPxP	N-B3
7. B-K3	. . .

If 7. N-KB3, B-N5 equalizes.

| 7. . . . | B-B4 |
| 8. N-QB3 | . . . |

Intending to defend against ... N-N5 with 9. R-B1.

| 8. ... | P-K3 |
| 9. N-B3 | B-K2 |

The normal line is 10. B-K2 0-0 11. 0-0 P-B3! and Black stirs up sufficient counter-chances.

| 10 P-Q5! | N-N5? |

Black should not avoid the following complications: 10. ... PxP 11. BxN RPxB 12. PxP N-N5 13. R-B1 NxRP 14. B-N5+ K-B1 (14. ... B-Q2 15. BxB+ QxB 16. R-R1!) 15. NxN RxN 16. Q-N3 R-R1 17. N-Q4 B-N3 18. P-Q6 PxP 19. N-K6+ PxN 20. 0-0+ B-B3, and Black holds by a hair, but he holds.

| 11. R-B1 | P-KB3 |

After 11. ... PxP, simply 12. P-QR3 anyway.

| 12. P-QR3 | N-R3 |
| 13. P-KN4! | ... |

The impact of such a move cannot be imagined, except by the person who happens to sit on the other side of the table. The "gambit" must be accepted, for if 13. ... B-N3, 14. PxKP wins a pawn.

13. ...	BxNP
41. R-KN1	P-KB4
15. P-R3	B-R5+
16. K-Q2!	B-R4

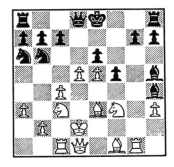

After 16. ... PxP 17. BxN BxN 18. Q-R4+ Q-Q2 19. QxQ+ KxQ 20. RxP+, Black is in grave difficulties. Black has chances after 16. ... PxP 17. PxB P-Q5 18. BxP P-B4.

17. RxP	PxP
18. PxP	NxP
19. Q-R4+	P-B3

If 19. ... K-B1, 20. B-R6(!).

20. QxB	BxN
21. B-KN5	Q-R4
22. P-N4!	

Black is lost. There may follow 22. ... QxRP 23. BxN! QxB 24. Q-R6 and there is no defense.

3. *Alekhine Defense*

Did he fall or was he pushed? "Sacrifice," urges the Temptor, who purchases yet another soul, for the unsuspecting first player will soon feel more than the heat of the Black counter-attack.

1. P-K4	N-KB3
2. P-K5	N-Q4
3. P-Q4	P-Q3
4. N-KB3	...

Not as impressive as the *four-pawn attack* (P-QB4 and P-KB4), but a good system nevertheless.

| 4. ... | P-KN3 |

A move currently favored and exploited by Grandmaster Lothar Schmid and former World Correspondence Champion Hans Berliner.

| 5. N-N5 | ... |

In this writer's opinion, a bluff; 5. P-B4 is preferable.

5. ...	PxP!
6. PxP	B-N2
7. B-QB4	...

There is no percentage in 7. P-QB4 N-N5 8. QxQ+ KxQ 9. NxP+ K-K1 10. NxR N-B7+!

| 7. ... | P-QB3 |
| 8. N-QB3 | ... |

Berliner was justly proud of his efforts in this game. After 8. P-B4 P-B3! 9. N-KB3 B-N5 and Black is very comfortable. Now the Satanic urgings commence!

| 8. ... | P-KR3 |

"Go, the enemy king begs for mercy."

9. NxP?	KxN
10. NxN	PxN
11. BxP+	K-K1
12. P-K6	...

This blockade doesn't always work! White's development lags so that he may fear for the *sacrificed* material. White could have tried 12. Q-Q3 B-B4 13. Q-N5+ N-B3 14. QxP QxB 15. QxR+ K-B2 16. Q-N7, but after ... QxNP Black should still win.

| 12. ... | R-B1 |

To simultaneously attack the king pawn and defend the knight pawn.

13. Q-N4	R-B3
14. Q-QB4	N-R3!
15. B-K3	Q-R4+
16. B-Q2	...

After 16. P-B3, N-B2 wins the king pawn.

| 16. ... | Q-N3! |

Too many threats!

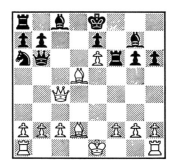

17. B-QB3	QxP+
18. K-Q1	BxP!!
19. BxR	...

If. 19. BxB, R-Q1+, 20. B-Q5, RxB+, 21. QxR, R-Q3 wins the Queen.

| 19. ... | R-Q1!! |
| 20. B-R4 | Q-N3 |

And Black can no longer be held at bay.

4. *Alekhine Defense*

Black's loss comes like toothpaste oozing from the tube—one minor misconception after another, without knowing exactly where the fatal blunder occurred.

1. P-K4	N-KB3
2. P-K5	N-Q4
3. N-QB3	NxN
4. NPxN	P-Q3
5. P-KB4	PxP?!

5. ... P-K3, and then B-K2 and 0-0 is much less appealing but also much more safe!

6. PxP	Q-Q4
7. P-Q4	P-QB4
8. N-B3	N-B3
9. B-K2	B-N5

10.	0-0	PxP
11.	PxP	P-K3
12.	R-N1!	Q-Q2
13.	N-N5!	BxB
14.	QxB	B-K2

Not 14. ... QxP+ 15. B-K3 QxP 16. NxBP! Instead Black sets a trap with the following flight of fancy as bait: 15. RxBP P-KR3 16. Q-R5 QxP+ 17. R-B2+ and White should win. However, after 15. RxBP QxP+ 16. B-K3 QxP, Black is quite snug. Or if 15. NxBP, 0-0! with advantage for Black.

15.	P-B3	BxN
16.	BxB	P-KR3
17.	B-B1!	. . .

Keeping an eye on the king rook pawn with a view to sacrifice, while retaining the option of B-R3.

17.	. . .	N-K2?!
18.	Q-B3	N-Q4?!
19.	P-B4	N-N3

The knight was much better on QB3.

| 20. | P-B5! | N-Q4 |
| 21. | P-B6! | . . . |

A *clearance* sacrifice opening a deadly diagonal for the queen bishop.

| 21. | . . . | PxP |
| 22. | B-R3 | P-KB4 |

With no decent prospects Black makes a break for it.

23. PxPe.p.	PxP
24. R-N3	K-Q1
25. KR-N1	R-R2

Hoping to obtain two rooks for the queen.

| 26. Q-N3! | N-N3 |

Closing the file?

| 27. RxN! | PxR |
| 28. Q-KN8+ | |

The queen rook is no longer defended, while on ... Q-K1, simply 29. QxR.

5. *Alekhine Defense*

For those enamored of the fianchetto, beware of the fast break—or is that basketball! Often one can neutralize the fianchetto (the development of a bishop on N2) by swapping off that bishop—at times even when it costs material to bring down the wily cleric.

| 1. P-K4 | N-KB3 |
| 2. N-QB3 | ... |

Best is still 2. P-K5.

2. ...	P-Q4!
3. PxP	NxP
4. KN-K2	...

The knight belongs on B3.

| 4. ... | N-QB3 |
| 5. P-KN3?? | B-N5! |

The pin is decisive. White had no plan and so a little trap will always be enough.

| | 6. B-N2 | N-Q5! |
| | 7. BxN | . . . |

Black threatened to win a piece by NxQN.

| | 7. . . . | QxB!! |
| | 8. P-B3 | . . . |

He should have played this on move seven.

The queen is taboo: 8. NxQ N-B6+ 9. K-B1 B-R6 mate. Or refuse the queen: 8. 0-0 N-B6+ 9. K-R1 N-N4+ 10. NxQ B-B6+ 11. K-N1 N-R6 mate.

| | 8. . . . | QxBP |
| | 9. R-B1 | Q-N7 |

And White has nothing but frustration.

6. *Caro-Kann Defense*

Never take the king rook pawn, even with check! This rule was tailor-made for this game alone. Black knows the rule but grows impatient. He gives up too much time for the gain of an unimportant pawn, and time is the commodity the defender does not have in abundance. The end is elegant!

1. P-K4	P-QB3
2. P-Q4	P-Q4
3. N-QB3	PxP
4. NxP	B-B4
5. N-N3	B-N3
6. B-QB4	P-K3
7. N(1)-K2	N-KB3
8. 0-0	B-Q3
9. P-B4	Q-B2

To neutralize White's plan Black should play 9. ... N-R4 10. P-B5 NxN 11. NxN (11. PxB? NxN+) PxP 12. NxP 0-0 and Black has a fighting chance. Unfortunately, he now casts a greedy eye on White's king rook pawn.

10. P-B5!	PxP
11. NxP	BxP+?

Castling offers greater resistance.

12. K-R1	0-0

Strange! Now castling is a mistake; 12. ... BxN was mandatory.

13. Q-K1	B-Q3

Defending against 14. P-KN3, but the position demanded 13. ... BxN first!

14. NxP!!	KxN
15. RxN!	N-Q2

If 15. ... KxR, then 16. Q-R4+ K-N2 17. B-R6+ K-N1 18. Q-B6!

16. Q-R4	KR-K1
17. B-R6+	K-R1
18. R(1)-KB1	Q-Q1
19. B-KN5	B-K2
20. RxB!!	Resigns.

After 20. ... PxR, 21. R-B7 decides.

7. *Caro-Kann Defense*

Diverting his knight from the center, Black falls prey to a peculiar brand of the pin. Offside with a steed, better take heed!

1. P-K4	P-QB3
2. P-Q4	P-Q4
3. N-QB3	PxP
4. NxP	B-B4
5. N-N3	B-N3
6. P-KR4	P-KR3
7. N-B3	N-Q2

Preventing 8. N-K5.

8. P-R5	B-R2
9. B-Q3	BxB
10. QxB	Q-B2
11. B-Q2	N(1)-B3
12. Q-K2	P-K3
13. 0-0-0	0-0-0
14. N-K5	N-N3?

Exchanging knights is far better than wandering afield with such a sturdy steed.

15. B-R5!	P-B4
16. P-QB4!	RxP
17. RxR	PxR
18. K-N1!	...

The White queen bishop pawn will not be harried by a pin as it hurries down the file!

| 18. ... | B-Q3 |
| 19. P-B5!! | ... |

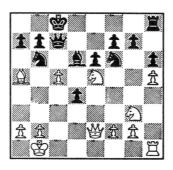

| 19. ... | BxN |

The pin enforced by the White queen bishop has been annoying; that of a White rook along the queen bishop file will be deadly.

| 20. PxN | PxP |
| 21. R-QB1 | Black resigns. |

If 21. ... PxB, then 22. QxB!

8. *Caro-Kann Defense*

One of the oldest yet least known traps in any opening is pictured here. The Mother of all Caro-Kann traps is so frequently successful because Black is usually unaware that White has saved a *tempo* by omitting P-Q4, developing his queen knight instead. *Voici*!

1. P-K4	P-QB3
2. N-QB3!	P-Q4
3. N-B3	PxP
4. NxP	B-B4
5. N-N3	B-N3?

Here we go! 5. . . . B-N5 was mandatory.

| **6. P-KR4!** | **P-KR3** |

Black must save his bishop.

7. N-K5!	**B-R2**
8. Q-R5!	**P-KN3**
9. Q-B3	**N-B3**

If Black prefers to trade queens, he loses material anyway: 9. . . . Q-Q4 10. QxQ! PxQ 11. B-N5+!

| **10. Q-N3!** | **Q-Q4** |

A pawn must go. The text is a futile attempt to save everything.

| **11. QxNP!!** | **QxN+** |
| **12. B-K2** | **Black resigns.** |

He must prevent 13. Q-B8 mate, whereupon he loses the rook in the corner.

9. *Caro-Kann Defense*

This fine trap was sprung in the semi-final round of an important tournament at eight o'clock in the morning! The theme is the blockade, preventing an opponent from getting to the cafeteria for his morning coffee!

1. P-K4	P-QB3
2. N-QB3	P-Q4
3. N-B3	P-KN3
4. P-Q4	B-N2
5. P-KR3	. . .

Restricting the development of Black's queen bishop.

5. . . .	PxP
6. NxP	B-B4?!
7. N-N3	N-B3

In the first place, Black should have postponed the development of his queen bishop; now he must cede a bishop for a knight to avoid loss of time.

8. NxB	Q-R4+
9. P-B3	QxN
10. Q-N3!	0-0?

This time the queen knight pawn may be taken! Black had no choice but to play the awkward Q-B1, safely tucking away the queen.

| 11. QxP! | QN-Q2 |
| 12. B-K2 | Q-K5 |

Black's dream of attack now becomes a nightmare. True, he has prevented White from castling, but castling is not always a necessity.

| 13. Q-R6! | . . . |

White threatens to complete his development by 0-0; so Black must take active measures, if he is to have any compensation for the pawn.

| 13. . . . | P-B4? |

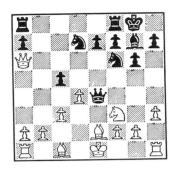

Active but catastrophic. Black may test White's ability to win with a pawn up with 13. ... P-R3.

14. N-N5!!

White wins at least the exchange, but he may also trap the queen. Observe! 14. ... Q-B4 (14. ... QxNP 15. B-B3 wins the queen.) 15. P-KN4! Q-B7 (15. ... Q-Q4 16. B-B3 wins the exchange.) 16. B-Q1!

10. *Caro-Kann Defense*

A mistake is usually just that, a mistake. The bait a delicacy, the trap a mirage. But when one imagines a trap, overly catering to his fears, a player inevitably walks into the real thing.

1. P-K4	P-QB3
2. P-Q4	P-Q4
3. PxP	PxP
4. P-QB4	. . .

The exchange of pawns, followed by this pawn advance, introduces the Botvinnik-Panov Attack.

| 4. . . . | N-KB3 |
| 5. B-N5? | . . . |

White waits for 5. ... P-K3 when there may follow 6. BxN QxB 7. PxP PxP 8. B-N5+ N-B3 9. N-QB3 B-K3 10. N-B3 B-K2 11. N-K5 QR-B1 12. Q-R4 with advantage to White. But White will wait a long time; correct was 5. N-QB3.

5. ...	N-K5!
6. B-K3	P-K4!
7. N-KB3	...

Or 7. Q or BPxP, B-N5+! anyway.

7. ...	B-N5+
8. QN-Q2	KPxP
9. NxP	Q-B3!

The threat is BxN+ and QxP mate.

| 10. Q-R4+ | N-B3 |
| 11. N-N3 | ... |

Castles long does not provide escape: 11: 0-0-0 BxN+ 12. BxB QxN.

| 11. ... | QxP |

After the exchange of all the pieces on Q2, Black picks up the loose rook.

| 12. R-Q1 | 0-0! |
| 13. PxP | N-B6 |

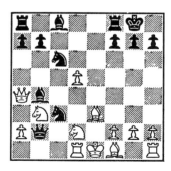

White's queen is ensconced.

11. *Caro-Kann Defense*

The *natural* move does not anticipate the hidden pin on the queen knight and, later, the queen rook pawn.

1. P-K4	P-QB3
2. P-Q4	P-Q4
3. PxP	PxP
4. P-QB4	N-KB3
5. N-QB3	N-B3
6. B-N5	. . .

The opening plan: steady attack on Black's queen pawn.

6. . . .	Q-R4
7. N-B3	. . .

After 7. BxN White feared . . . KPxB 8. PxP N-N5 9. B-B4 B-KB4!

7. . . .	B-N5
8. BxN	KPxB
9. PxP	B-N5!
10. Q-N3	. . .

A mating net is woven after 10. PxN BxN+ 11. PxB QxP+ 12. K-K2 0-0!

10. . . .	BxKN
11. PxN	. . .

Not 11. PxB NxP!

11. . . .	BxBP
12. B-B4?	. . .

Oh for 12. P-QR3! Does the text gain a tempo by hitting the king bishop pawn? Yes! But sadly, it also puts the White queen on the spot.

12. ...	B-R5!
13. BxP+	K-B1
14. Q-B4	B-N4
15. Q-N3	...

The queen must fend off ... BxN+.

| 15. ... | R-Q1 |

Neither can White castle queen side: 16. 0-0-0 BxN 17. PxB B-R5!

16. P-QR4	RxP!
17. P-B4	BxRP!
18. RxB	QxR!
19. QxQ	BxN+

Recovering the queen with a decisive material edge.

12. *Caro-Kann Defense*

The magic of Tal puts shivers in the timbers.

1. P-K4	P-QB3
2. P-Q4	P-Q4
3. PxP	PxP
4. P-QB4	N-KB3

5. N-QB3	P-K3
6. N-B3	B-K2
7. PxP	...

Or 7. B-Q3 8. 0-0 PxP 9. BxP 0-0 with equality.

7. ...	NxP
8. B-Q3	N-QB3
9. 0-0	0-0
10. P-QR3	...

Anticipating ... N(3)-N5 followed by ... NxN and the posting of the new knight on Q4.

10. ...	NxN
11. PxN	B-B3

Better is ... P-QN3, B-N2 and R-B1.

12 Q-K2	B-Q2
13. R-N1	P-QN3
14. R-K1	R-K1
15. P-KR4	...

A friendly pawn offer; if now 15. ... BxRP, 16. Q-K4!

15. ...	P-K4?

Inopportune, since the White queen will not remain to be buffeted about on the open file. The same idea is possible after 15. ... P-KN3, although White is definitely better.

16. N-N5!	...

Now . . . P-KN3 is met by 17. P-Q5! Yet this is the only move.

16. . . .	PxP
17. BxP+	K-B1
18. B-K4	BxN

After 18. . . . PxP 19. Q-R5 P-N3 20. Q-R7 B-N2 21. NxP! KxN 22. BxP+ K-B1 23. B-R6, mate is unavoidable.

| 19. BxB | P-B3 |

Or else 20. Q-R5 also mates.

| 20. Q-R5 | RxB |

If . . . PxB, simply 21. B-Q5.

| 21. RxR | K-N1 |

Or 21. . . . PxB 22. PxNP K-N1 23. P-N6!

22. B-Q2	B-K1
23. Q-KB5	B-B2
24. R-KN4	K-R1
25. R-K1	

White has the exchange and a powerful attack.

13. *Caro-Kann Defense*

Basic to this opening line is the development of the queen bishop. White bluffs with 7. B-QB4, gesturing at KB7. Black, a noted grandmaster, fails to call the bluff and locks in his bishop with the unfortunate 7. . . . P-K3

1. P-K4	P-QB3
2. P-Q4	P-Q4
3. N-QB3	PxP
4. NxP	N-B3?

We affix the *inferior* sign not because the text loses by force but because theory considers the text worse than B-B4, N-Q2, or even P-KN3. Desiring complications, Black submits to a rupture of his pawn structure.

| 5. NxN+! | NPxN |

Fast development is afforded by ... KPxN, after which Black, of course, must avoid most endings, since practically speaking he is a pawn down.

| 6. P-QB3 | Q-B2 |
| 7. B-QB4! | P-K3?? |

Correct is 7 ... B-B4.

| 8. Q-R5! | P-QB4 |

Now Black cannot continue normally, for if 8. ... N-Q2, 9. BxP(!), enforces a deadly pin.

| 9. P-Q5 | P-K4 |
| 10. N-K2 | B-Q3 |

Necessary is 10. ... N-Q2, and if 11. P-Q6, then QxP 12. QxP+ K-Q1 securing the king to the queen side.

| 11. P-B4 | N-Q2 |

Too late for salvation; there is no time to oust White's king bishop.

| 12. 0-0 | P-QR3 |
| 13. P-QN3 | N-N3? |

13. ... P-N4 is better but White should win anyway.

| 14. PxP | PxP |

After 14. ... BxP, 15. P-Q6!

15. N-N3	NxB
16. PxN	P-N3
17. N-K4	R-R2

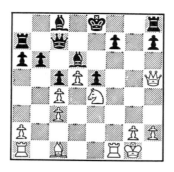

It's all over now!

18. RxP!

Black loses his queen: 18. . . . QxR 19. NxB+!

14. *Caro-Kann Defense*

The theme crops up again: the central pawn speeding to the sixth rank to choke the enemy development.

1.	P-K4	P-QB3
2.	P-Q4	P-Q4
3.	P-K5	. . .

An idea analyzed by Weaver Adams, popularized by Grandmaster Arthur Bisguier and, finally, reaching Mount Olympus, utilized by World Champion Mikhail Botvinnik in his second title match with Latvian Grandmaster Mikhail Tal. White tempts Black to develop his queen bishop prematurely whereupon White will extort time for the attack by prodding His Grace with the king side pawns.

| 3. . . . | B-B4?! |

Botvinnik later found 3. . . . P-QB4 to be better.

| 4. P-KN4 | B-Q2 |

Alekhine recommended 4. ... B-K5; Botvinnik and David Bronstein actually played the text. Let the reader take his choice; both moves seem playable.

5. B-Q3	Q-B1
6. P-KR3	P-QB4
7. P-QB3	N-QB3
8. B-K3	PxP
9. BxQP	...

So as not to remain with a bishop locked behind his own pawns.

9. ...	Q-B2
10. P-KB4!	NxB
11. PxN	Q-N3

Black nibbles at the bait; he should play 11. ... P-K3.

12. Q-Q2	...

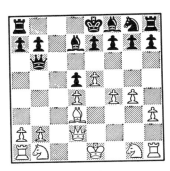

Defending the queen pawn, and waiting. ...

12. ...	QxQP??

After 12. ... P-K3 White has some initiative but hardly a won game.

13. P-K6!	...

A very sudden end. After 13. ... BxP, 14. B-N5+ wins the queen, and after 14. ... B-B3, a pawn promotes to the highest honor: 15. PxP+ K-Q1 (15. ... KxP 16. B-N6+!) 16. PxN=Q!

29

15. *Caro-Kann Defense*

Always check, it might be mate. Relying on such a principle
leads to poor moves, which in turn spells doom. This one is
an oldie but a goodie!

1. **P-K4**	**P-QB3**
2. **P-Q4**	**P-Q4**
3. **P-KB3**	**PxP**

Whatever is best against White's strange debut, the text
isn't the answer—probably P-K3.

4. PxP   **P-K4**

Remember the King's Gambit trap: 1. P-K4 P-K4 2. P-KB4
N-QB3 3. PxP? Q-R5+!

5. N-KB3   **PxP**

To prevent the incursion of White's king bishop Black should
try 5. ... B-K3, for if 6. NxP, then ... Q-R5+.

6. B-QB4   **B-N5+**

We consistently recommend simple development: 6. ...
N-B3, B-K2 and 0-0.

7. P-B3!   **PxP?**

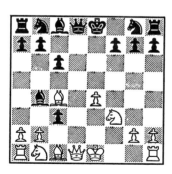

Now ... B-R4 or B-K2 is a must, but Black is unaware of
the net White has woven.

8. BxP+!	KxB

8. ... K-K2, offers resistance, but Black thinks he is winning.

9. QxQ	PxP+
10. K-K2	PxR=Q
11. N-N5+	K-N3
12. Q-K8+	K-R3
13. N-K6+	P-N4
14. BxP	

Black has been checkmated.

16. *Center-Counter*

Double pawn—Double strength! That's what one says to console oneself, having been saddled with this particular weakness. If anyone is faithful to that pseudo-dictum, Fischer will help him become an infidel.

1. P-K4	P-Q4
2. PxP	QxP

The instant recapture has fallen out of favor. Theory suggests 2. ... N-KB3 3. P-QB4?! P-B3!—offering a pawn for rapid development, control of Q5, and the opportunity to prey on White's backward queen pawn. White may conveniently decline the sac with 4. P-Q4! PxP 5. N-QB3.

3. N-QB3	Q-Q1

More aggressive, but also more dangerous, is Q-QR4.

4. P-Q4	N-KB3
5. B-QB4	B-B4?

White counts on his opponent's knowledge that every manual demands Black develop this bishop, for here we have the exception.

6. Q-B3!	Q-B1
7. B-N5!	BxP?

How many mistakes can a bishop make?

8. R-QB1	B-N3
9. KN-K2	QN-Q2
10. 0-0	P-K3
11. BxN!!	PxB?

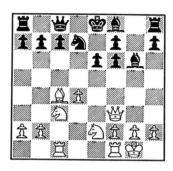

On 11. ... NxB, 12. P-Q5 is still strong. Black does continue to live after 12. ... B-Q3 13. PxP 0-0! Now for a few death-dealing blows!

12. P-Q5!	P-K4
13. B-N5!	B-K2
14. N-N3	P-QR3
15. B-Q3	Q-Q1
16. P-KR4	P-KR4
17. B-B5!	N-N3
18. N(B3)-K4	NxP
19. KR-Q1	P-B3
20. N-B3	Q-N3
21. RxN!!	PxR
22. NxQP	QxP
23. R-N1	QxP
24. RxP	

And Black gives up the ghost.

17. *Center-Counter*

This is not only an offbeat but an inferior opening. Yet, when used for the element of surprise, it can be a very effective weapon. In this case though, the burden of proof always rests with Black. In our example Black forgets to count the pieces before entering into complicated combinations. He snatches the poisoned pawn, but never again—in this game!

1.	P-K4	P-Q4
2.	PxP	QxP
3.	N-QB3	Q-QR4
4.	P-Q4	P-K4

Played in the hope of achieving quick equality. Black should play N-KB3 followed by P-B3, preparing a convenient retreat for his queen.

5.	N-KB3	B-QN5
6.	B-Q2	B-N5
7.	B-K2	N-QB3
8.	P-QR3	BxKN
9.	BxB	NxP?

Black spots the combination but doesn't spot the flaw. Correct though cumbersome is 10. .... B-Q3. There may follow 10. N-Q5 Q-N4! 11. P-QR4 Q-B5 12. PxP NxP 13. N-K3 NxB+ 14. QxN Q-R3 and White is only slightly better.

10.	PxB!	QxR

Now Black has no choice. He soon realizes his tricky play loses two pieces for a rook.

| 11. QxQ | NxP+ |
| 12. K-K2! | . . . |

Probably the simple move Black had not considered. It is often difficult to see that a piece is indirectly protected by a veil. In this instance the White king is the veil which when moved from the first to the second rank allows the king rook to defend the queen rook.

The type of combination witnessed here is marked by the surrender of material. The plan is to regain the material and even something more by employing a gain-of-time motif, usually by checking the king or attacking a major piece. Unfortunately for Black, the combination does not work in this situation.

12. . . .	NxQ
13. RxN	P-QB3
14. B-K3	N-K2
15. B-B5	P-B4
16. K-K3!	. . .

Accurate play is still necessary, even to the extent of seemingly placing one's king in danger. When the king goes forward he does not block the backward movements of his king bishop.

| 16. . . . | P-QR3 |
| 17. P-N5! | . . . |

With this breakthrough, made possible by the pin along the queen rook file, White is able to begin a mating attack, an attack all the more unusual because the queens have already been exchanged.

17. . . .	P-K5
18. B-K2	BPxP
19. NxNP	P-B5+
20. KxKP!	0-0

21. N-Q6	P-QN4
22. B-KN4!	P-N3

Black tries to set up a post for his knight to screen out White's king bishop. But it is too late; White wraps up a pretty finish.

23. B-K6+	K-N2
24. B-Q4+	K-R3
25. N-B7+	K-R4
26. R-R3!!	Resigns.

18. *Center-Counter*

Now it is Black's turn to spring the trap in almost the same setting.

1. P-K4	P-Q4
2. PxP	QxP
3. N-QB3	Q-QR4
4. P-Q4	P-K4
5. PxP?!	B-QN5
6. B-Q2	N-QB3
7. P-QR3	N-Q5?!

Will he catch the lion asleep in his lair? 7. .... QxP+ leads to a level game.

8. PxB??	...

Correct was 8. P-B4 B-KB4 9. R-B1 and Black goes begging for his pawn.

| 8. ... | QxR! |
| 9. QxQ | NxP+ |

The pesky knight picks up the queen and hops out via QN6.

19. *Danish Gambit*

The opening is played with a certain lack of finesse on both sides. Yet we note that perfection has no monopoly over beauty. A master does not lose unless he errs. Here White devises a worthy trap to ensnare even the greatest grandmaster.

1. P-K4	P-K4
2. P-Q4	PxP
3. P-QB3	PxP
4. B-QB4	N-QB3

Theory holds that Black may equalize after 4. ... PxP 5. BxP P-Q4! 6. BxQP N-KB3 7. BxP+ KxB 8. QxQ B-N5+ 9. QN-Q2 RxQ.

| 5. P-QR3 | QN-K2? |

There are still other pieces to develop!

| 6. N-B3 | P-QR3? |

While White has time for a move like P-QR3, Black does not.

7. 0-0	P-QN4
8. B-R2	P-QB3
9. N-N5	N-R3
10. Q-N3	Q-R4
11. R-K1!!	...

For Black an irresistible temptation to gain material.

| 11. ... | PxP? |
| 12. R-Q1! | PxR=Q |

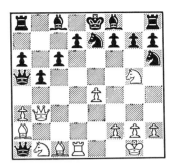

13. QxP+!	NxQ
14. BxN+	K-Q1
15. N-K6	Black has been checkmated!

20. *Evans Gambit*

Gambits in the old style seem to have all but disappeared.
But, be prepared! Chess is constantly evolving. When wood-
pushers tire of the currently-in-vogue hypermodern debuts,
they will look for new enjoyment in the sparkle of the old
gambits.

1. P-K4	P-K4
2. N-KB3	N-QB3
3. B-B4	B-B4
4. P-QN4	BxP
5. P-B3	B-R4
6. P-Q4	PxP

The Evans Gambit had temporarily fallen out of favor
mainly due to Lasker's Defense: 6. ... P-Q3 7. 0-0 B-N3! after
which Black maintains a sturdy center. We might note that
White still has fine attacking prospects whatever the defense
adopted.

| 7. 0-0 | N-B3 |

Preferable is 7. ... B-N3; but the text is playable.

| 8. PxP | 0-0? |

Running from the fight doesn't help. Either 8. ... P-Q3 or Q4 was mandatory.

| 9. P-K5 | N-K1?? |

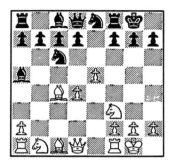

Indeed Black had the worse game but his only chance was to stand and fight with 9. ... P-Q4!

| 10. P-Q5 | N-K2 |
| 11. P-Q6! | N-N3?? |

One final slip was necessary; 11. ... PxP would give Black's queen some fresh air.

| 12. B-KN5 |

To save his queen Black must interpose his knight losing this piece. He resigns with his position in tatters.

21. *French Defense*

The whole defense is based upon the possibility of capturing the QN Pawn. Soon Black sees there is no defense, for if he should take the pawn of legendary fame, his queen would be trapped!

| 1. P-K4 | P-K3 |
| 2. P-Q4 | P-Q4 |

3. N-QB3	B-N5
4. P-K5	P-QB4
5. Q-N4	N-K2
6. PxP	QN-B3

White has refused the KN Pawn fearful of giving Black some initiative. Black so far has exercised correct judgment, but he may also incorrectly encourage such a capture: 6. ... BxN 7. PxB N-Q2 8. QxNP! R-KN1 9. QxP Q-B2 10. N-K2 with a clear edge for White.

7. B-Q2	N-B4
8. N-B3	BxP
9. B-Q3	0-0

Castling is too dangerous—almost self-mate! Black should secure his king knight with P-KR4.

10. B-KN5!	Q-N3
11. 0-0	Q-N5

An aimless wandering, hoping for the exchange of queens. Better is B-K2. A clever way to lose may be seen in: 11. ... BxP+ 12. RxB QxP 13. QR-KB1 QxN 14. B-B6 K-R1 15. BxN NPxB 16. BxRP KxB 17. N-N5+ PxN 18. Q-R5+!! with unavoidable mate.

12. Q-R3	P-KR3
13. P-R3!!	...

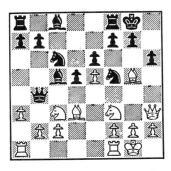

Taking the NP loses the queen to N-QR4!

13. ...	Q-N3
14. BxN!	KPxB
15. NxP	QxP

Too late!

16. N-B6+	PxN
17. BxBP	K-R2
18. Q-R5!!	

The threat of N-N5+(!) is just too much.

22. *French Defense*

Jittery nerves surely are the real enemy here. Anxious to divert White's forces from the attack, Black forgets that bishops do indeed move forward.

1. P-K4	P-K3
2. P-Q4	P-Q4
3. N-QB3	N-KB3
4. B-N5	B-K2
5. P-K5	N-K5

The normal tactic is N-Q2 followed by N-QB3 and P-KB3 with pressure against the pawn center.

| 6. BxB | QxB |
| 7. Q-N4 | 0-0 |

The castling maneuver is possible because White's queen bishop is out of the way.

8. B-Q3	NxN
9. PxN	P-QB4
10. N-B3	...

The stage is set. White already has strong pressure owing to his lead in development, but he still needs some help to pull off a smashing victory.

| 10. ... | P-B5?? |

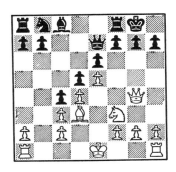

Defense is offered by P-KR3 combined with N-Q2 and P-B4.
They used to say that *three pieces are a mate!*

| 11. BxP+!! | . . . |

After 11. ... KxB 12. N-N5+ K-N1 13. Q-R5, Black must
play QxN to avoid checkmate!

23. *French Defense*

"The queen knight pawn is taboo," this much is known. But
cannot a player indulge just a little and snatch the king rook
pawn?

1. P-K4	P-K3
2. P-Q4	P-Q4
3. N-QB3	B-N5
4. Q-N4	. . .

A sharp move and therefore a favorite of Mikhail Tal,
ex-world champion.

4. ...	N-KB3
5. QxP!	R-N1
6. Q-R6	NxP
7. QxP?	. . .

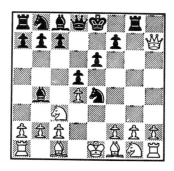

Gaining a tempo on the rook but losing the game. Munching on a stray pawn may be considered an epicurean delight but one can have too much of a good thing. Correct was either KN-K2 or B-Q2.

| 7. ... | R-B1 |
| 8. B-Q2 | BxN!! |

In this instance the knight is more important than the bishop.

| 9 BxB | Q-B3! |

The combined threats against KB2 and the queen (R-R1!) force White's resignation.

24. French Defense

The setting is the Tournament of Peace, Zagreb, Yugoslavia, 1970. In an earlier round Bobby Fischer had *brilliantly* upended Grandmaster Wolfgang Uhlmann, but the experts questioned Bobby's opening analysis. Vladimir Kovacevic of Yugoslavia has gone to the drawing boards and found the flaw in the line. Thereafter, the gods had decreed that the great Bobby was to be enmeshed in his own web!

1. P-K4	P-K3
2. P-Q4	P-Q4
3. N-QB3	B-N5

| 4. P-QR3 | BxN+ |
| 5. PxB | PxP |

In capturing the pawn, Black is well aware that he must return same, but he relies on the better bargain, gaining a central pawn for a flank colleague.

6. Q-N4	N-KB3
7. QxNP	R-N1
8. Q-R6	QN-Q2
9. N-K2	P-N3!

The immediate attack on the center, 9. ... P-B4, favors White, whose bishop pair will operate effectively on an open board.

| 10. B-N5 | ... |

10. B-N2 followed by 0-0-0 is more reliable.

| 10. ... | Q-K2 |

Now White cannot castle long since his queen rook pawn hangs.

11. Q-R4	B-N2
12. N-N3	P-KR3!
13. B-Q2	...

The ignominious retreat is a direct consequence of a very careless tenth move. White cannot play 13. QxRP because of 13. ... 0-0-0, menacing R-R1.

13. ...	0-0-0
14. B-K2	N-B1
15. 0-0	N-N3
16. QxRP	R-R1
17. Q-N5	...

Black wins easily after 17. Q-K3 N-Q4 18. QxP N(4)-B5.

| 17. ... | QR-N1 |
| 18. P-B3 | P-K6! |

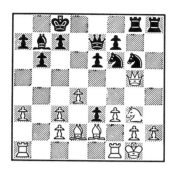

The attack rolls after this pawn sac; 18. ... PxP frees White's game, giving him the king bishop file to boot.

19. BxP · · ·

Or 19. QxP N-Q4 20. Q-B2 Q-R5(!).

19. ...	**N-B1**
20. Q-N5	**N-Q4**

Locking out the queen from the defense of the king.

21. K-B2 · · ·

The king tries to flee his burning castle, but the drawbridge has already collapsed.

21. ... **P-R3!**

Denying any possibility of Q-K8.

22. Q-Q3	**RxP**
23. R-R1	**Q-R5!**
24. RxR	**QxR**
25. N-B1	**RxP+**
26. K-K1	**Q-R5+**
27. K-Q2	**N-N3**
28. R-K1	**N(3)-B5**
29. BxN	**NxB**
30. Q-K3	**R-B7!**

Black cannot handle the threats of . . . BxP and . . . N-N7.

25. *French Defense*

The second player's penchant for originality gets him in trouble. He surely knows the tried and true 7. ... Q-N3. He has also been taught to attack swiftly the strongpoint K5. He stubbornly applies the lesson of the past without regard to existing conditions. Neglecting sound development, he falls prey to violent retribution.

1.	P-K4	P-K3
2.	P-Q4	P-Q4
3.	N-Q2	N-KB3
4.	P-K5	KN-Q2
5.	B-Q3	P-QB4
6.	P-QB3	QN-B3
7.	N-K2	P-B3?
8.	N-KB4!	Q-K2
9.	N-B3	PxKP
10.	N-N6!!	. . .

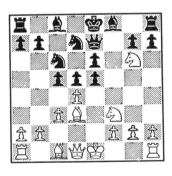

Not a sacrifice in the strict sense, since Black must accept!

10.	. . .	PxN
11.	BxP+	K-Q1
12.	B-N5	N-B3

In fact, no sacrifice at all!
Black must voluntarily enter a pin to save his queen.

45

13. PxKP	K-B2
14. 0-0	B-Q2
15. P-QN4!	P-B5

Just as Black regroups, White pries open another sector, enhancing the activity of his more mobile forces.

16. P-N5!!	N-QR4
17. R-K1	Q-Q1
18. Q-Q4	B-K2

The pin is broken—too late!

| 19. PxN | PxP |
| 20. B-B4+ | K-B1 |

If 20. ... P-K4, then 21. NxP PxN 22. BxP+!

21. B-KB7!	P-K4
22. NxP!!	PxN
23. QxKP	B-QB4
24. QxP	Q-N3
25. QR-Q1!!	

Black must resign!

26. *French Defense*

Castle if you must, if you wish to, but don't castle merely because you are able!

1. P-K4	P-K3
2. P-Q4	P-Q4
3. N-Q2	P-QB4
4. KN-B3	N-QB3
5. PxQP	QxP
6. B-B4	Q-B4?!

Better to return home. The queen will be exposed to attack on the open board.

7. 0-0	N-B3
8. N-N3	P-QR3
9. R-K1	. . .

White forces his opponent to lose time either by capturing the queen pawn when White recaptures with an attack on the queen, or by moving his king bishop when that bishop will have to move again to capture on QB4.

9. . . .	B-K2
10. NxP!	BxN
11. B-Q3!	Q-R4
12. PxB	0-0??

Black must immediately recapture the pawn and then develop his queen side with P-QN4 and B-N2.

13. B-KB4!	. . .

Surprise! The pawn is lost forever.

13. . . .	QxP??

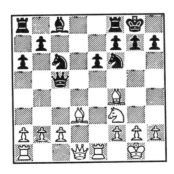

14. B-Q6!!

Black loses the exchange. Naturally if 14. ... QxB, 15. BxP+—because Black is castled!—wins the queen.

27. French Defense

Push back the enemy! Blind application of this principle puts Black in the soup. Patience is always the password. Instead of forcing the knight away with 9. . . . P-KR3(?), Black, by this impetuous gesture, leaves himself open to a sparkling sacrifice!

1. P-K4	P-K3
2. P-Q4	P-Q4
3. N-Q2	P-QN3?!

Unusual, but not bad.

4. KN-B3	PxP
5. NxP	B-N2
6. B-Q3	N-KB3
7. Q-K2	QN-Q2
8. 0-0	B-K2
9. N(4)-N5!	P-KR3?

Just what White wanted! Necessary and good was 9. . . . 0-0.

10. NxKP!!	PxN
11. B-N6+	K-B1
12. P-B4!!	. . .

A preventive measure; if 12. QxP, B-Q4!

12. ...	B-Q3
13. QxP	Q-K2
14. Q-R3	Q-K7

There is no relief after 14. ... N-K5 15. R-K1 N(2)-B3 16. Q-R4 K-N1 17. P-Q5! Or 14. ... BxN 15. QxB R-QN1 16. B-Q2, followed by 17. QR-K1.

15. R-K1	QxBP
16. N-K5!	Q-Q4
17. B-B4	R-Q1
18. N-B7!	BxB
19. NxQR	N-B4
20. PxN	QxN
21. QR-Q1	B-Q4
22. RxB!!	NxR
23. Q-K6	

Black resigns just in time!

28. *Hedgehog Defense*

In the last century, before the development of modern opening theory, a mode of defense, Hedgehog by name, became semi-popular. We say semi because only players with suitable styles would venture such a risky system. By placing all his pawns on the third rank a player dares his opponent, "Come and get me!" The defender voluntarily traps himself in a cramped position in the hope that his opponent will err in the conduct of the attack.

1. P-K4	P-Q3
2. P-Q4	N-KB3
3. N-QB3	P-KN3
4. B-K2	B-N2
5. P-KR4	P-N3?!

Better alternatives are P-B3, P-B4, QN-Q2, N-B3 or P-KR4.

| 6. B-B3! | P-B3 |
| 7. P-R5 | P-QR3?! |

The typical position of the Hedgehog. White uses only a small pin to crack this nut—anyone who adopts such a system!

| 8. PxP | BPxP? |

Capturing towards the center is elementary.

| 9. B-K3 | QN-Q2?? |

Why not start developing the right piece now? B-K3, Q-B2 and then QN-Q2 and possibly 0-0-0 offer good defensive chances.

| 10. P-K5! | PxP |
| 11. BxP | R-QN1? |

Black must give up a rook for a minor piece with ... PxP.

| 12. PxP | N-R4 |
| 13. P-K6 | |

Again and again this winning thrust comes up.

29. *Hungarian Defense*

This opening has been dubbed the "safe" defense. No doubt the defender in this game relies heavily on its reputation, and indulges in the time-wasting maneuver N-QR3-B2. True the Yugoslav Grandmaster, Gligorić employs such a tactic in the Yugoslav Variation of the King's Indian Defense, but this is not the King's Indian Defense.

1. P-K4	P-K4
2. N-KB3	N-QB3
3. B-B4	B-K2?!
4. P-Q4	P-Q3

The defense envisions exchanging queens, 5. PxP PxP 6. QxQ+ BxQ with approximate equality.

5. P-Q5!!	. . .

Considered one of White's best. Rossolimo recommends 5. P-KR3 N-B3 6. PxP! PxP 7. QxQ+ BxQ 8. N-B3 0-0 9. B-K3 B-K2 10. P-R3 and White stands better. However, after 8. . . . N-Q5, the position is unclear.

5. . . .	N-N1
6. B-Q3!	. . .

Preventing the freeing 6. . . . P-KB4.

6. .	P-QB4?!

The pawn formation is now identical to that of the Old Benoni with Black a tempo behind.

7. N-B3	N-QR3?

Better to proceed with N-KB3 and 0-0 intending immediate action on the king side. Further loss of time is disastrous.

8. N-Q2	N-B2
9. P-QR4	. . .

Precluding Black's P-QN4.

9. . . .	B-Q2
10. 0-0	P-QN3
11. N-B4	. . .

In the Old Benoni a white pawn occupies this square, here the knight dominates the board from the same post.

11. ...	R-N1

We could say, "Fiddling while Rome burns," but unfortunately the damage is already done.

12. P-B4!	...

Opening the position to profit from superior development.

12. ...	P-B3
13. PxP	BPxP
14. Q-R5+!	P-N3

After this the king side dark squares are a disaster area, but Black had no choice.

15. Q-B3	B-QB1

After 15. ... N-B3 comes 16. NxQP+!

16. Q-B7+	

Now there follows 16. ... K-Q2 17. Q-N7 N-B3 18. RxN R-N1 19. RxP+ winning easily.

30. King's Gambit

Every now and again the King's Gambit makes its presence felt in current opening theory. In this game, both sides cruise

52

to a common theoretical position (move 8.). The chances are even when White tries to make a quick profit. He finds he is in the wrong business.

1. P-K4	P-K4
2. P-KB4	PxP
3. N-KB3	P-KN4
4. P-KR4	P-N5
5. N-K5	N-KB3!

This solid defense takes the sting out of the Kieseritzky Gambit.

6. B-B4	. . .

A venerable but unclear line is 6. P-Q4 P-Q3 7. N-Q3 NxP 8. BxP Q-K2 9. Q-K2 B-N2 10. P-B3 and only practical play will determine whether White's development or Black's pawn will be of greater value.

6. . . .	P-Q4
7. PxP	B-Q3
8. P-Q4	N-R4!

All the books give 9. 0-0 QxP 10. Q-K1 QxQ 11. RxQ 0-0 with an even game.

9. NxNP??	N-N6!
10. R-R2	Q-K2+!!
11. K-B2	P-KR4!!!

53

One, two, three exclamation marks and White surrenders:
12. N-K5 BxN 13. PxB Q-B4+ and a piece goes.

31. *Pirc Defense*

Lured into a false attack by the prospect of material gain,
White witnesses his own demise accomplished by the Black
queen bishop pawn which terrorizes the White camp.

1. P-K4	P-Q3
2. P-Q4	N-KB3
3. N-QB3	P-KN3
4. P-B4	B-N2
5. N-B3	P-B4

White should proceed with 6. PxP! Q-R4 7. N-Q2 maintaining a slight edge.

6. B-N5+	B-Q2
7. P-K5	N-N5!
8. BxB+	QxB
9. N-KN5?	. . .

Necessary was 9. PxQP.

| 9. . . . | BPxP |
| 10. P-K6? | . . . |

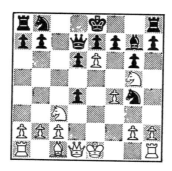

The reader must judge when to employ this stock thrust.
Here White's in for a little surprise.

10. ...	PxP
11. QxN	PxN
12. NxKP	...

All according to plan. But whose plan? Imperative was 12. P-QN3.

12. ...	PxP
13. NxB+	K-B2!

Now no options remain. Both the White queen and queen rook hang.

14. QxQ	PxB=Q+!!
15. RxQ	NxQ

And White's hapless knight cannot escape.

32. *Pirc Defense*

Black longs to break the chains that bind him. The resulting impetuosity runs him right into a brutal chain-reaction. The White knight menaces mate and then leisurely hops back to lop off the forward passed pawn, Black's last stronghold.

1. P-K4	P-Q3
2. P-Q4	N-KB3
3. N-QB3	P-KN3
4. P-B4	B-N2
5. N-B3	P-B4
6. PxP	Q-R4
7. B-Q3	QxBP
8. Q-K2	0-0
9. B-K3	Q-B2
10. 0-0	QN-Q2?!

So far, old hat. A possible improvement is 10. ... B-N5. To alleviate a cramped position one should indulge in the methodical exchange of pieces.

11. P-KR3!	P-QR3
12. P-QR4	P-N3
13. Q-B2	B-N2
14. Q-R4	N-B4
15. P-B5!	P-QN4

A trap that boomerangs.

16. RPxP	RPxP
17. NxP!	Q-Q2
18. RxR	RxR
19. BxN!	PxP

A zwischenzug intended to refute the attack, e.g., 20. PxP PxB and the bishops of opposite colors provide excellent play.

20. NxQP!	PxN
21. B-Q4	PxP
22. N-N5	PxB
23. BxN	P-R3
24. BxB	Q-B3
25. Q-B2	QxP+
26. QxQ	BxQ
27. KxB	KxB
28. N-B3	PxP
29. R-B1	R-QB1
30. N-K1	

White keeps the extra piece.

33. *Pirc Defense*

The end is so abrupt that the amateur hardly perceives his mistake—assuming that there was but one mistake.

1. P-K4	P-Q3	
2. P-Q4	N-KB3	
3. N-QB3	P-KN3	
4. B-N5	B-N2	
5. Q-Q2	P-B3	
6. 0-0-0	Q-R4	

The alignment of the White queen and rook should signal immediate danger; Black should castle.

7. N-B3	P-QN4?

The king pleads for safety— . . . 0-0!

8. P-K5!	P-N5??

The chain-reaction theme—each side capturing pieces successively with a pernicious pawn. Whoever forces the opponent to break his own chain wins. 8. . . . N-N1 is distasteful but the only hope.

9. PxN	PxN

Gardez la dame!

10. QxP!!	. . .

Gardez à vous too!

10. . . .	QxQ

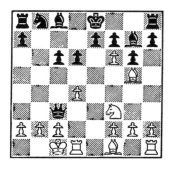

11. PxB!   . . .

The end of the rainbow. The rook must move whereupon White simply recaptures the queen with a piece up.

34. *Pirc Defense*

Black's overwhelming desire is to establish a King's-Indian type position with a strongpoint on K4. In this case White has no objections.

1. P-K4	P-Q3
2. P-Q4	N-KB3
3. N-QB3	P-B3
4. N-B3	P-KN3

Much too routine, since Black is prepared for the more normal development of B-KN5, followed by QN-Q2 and P-K4. Black may even choose the solid P-K3 and P-Q4, establishing the pawns on the white squares to compensate for the loss of the services of his queen bishop.

5. B-K2	B-N2
6. 0-0	0-0
7. P-KR3(!)	. . .

Presenting Black with the problem of developing his queen bishop.

| 7. ... | QN-Q2 |
| 8. B-K3 | P-K4? |

We shall see immediately why ... Q-B2 is better.

9. PxP!	PxP
10. Q-Q6!	R-K1
11. B-QB4!	Q-K2
12. QxQ	RxQ
13. P-QR4!	...

Now Black's position is as tight as a drum.

13. ...	P-N3
14. KR-Q1	B-N2
15. R-Q6	P-QR3
16. R(1)-Q1	P-QN4
17. B-N3	...

Exchanging pawns at this juncture only frees Black's game.

| 17. ... | P-R3 |
| 18. P-N4 | ... |

Perhaps 18. ... N-B1 offers greater resistance, but ...

18. ...	R-QB1
19. P-N5!	PxP
20. NxKNP	R-B2

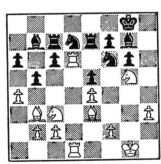

A "defensive" maneuver that costs the game.

| 21. P-R5! | ... |

The threat B-N6 panics the defender.

21. ...	K-B1?
22. BxP	RxB
23. N-K6+	K-N1
24. NxR	B-KB1
25. N-K8!	K-R2
26. RxN(7)!	...

After ... NxR 27. RxN RxR 28. N-B6+, White emerges with an extra piece.

35. *Pirc Defense*

Black attempts to cure the wanderlust of the White king knight.

1. P-K4	P-Q3
2. P-Q4	P-KN3
3. N-QB3	B-N2
4. B-K3	N-KB3
5. P-B3	...

A similar position is reached in the Saemisch Attack of the King's Indian Defense. The difference: there is no pawn at QB4 in the Pirc. That is sometimes good, sometimes bad. The individual player must make the judgment.

5. ...	P-B3

Providing a post at Q4 for the king knight, should White play P-K5.

6. Q-Q2	P-KR4

A complete waste of time.

7. 0-0-0	P-QN4
8. KN-K2	Q-R4
9. N-B4	...

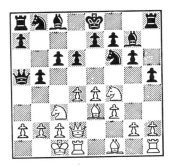

There is no immediate threat; so there is time for 9. . . . QN-Q2. Unfortunately, Black is spellbound by what appears to be an errant knight.

9. . . .	P-K4?
10. PxP	PxP
11. Q-Q6!	KN-Q2

Take it or leave it, 11. . . . PxN that is: 12. B-B5 B-B1 13. QxN(6) BxB 14. QxR+!!

12. N(4)-Q5!	PxN
13. NxQP	B-B1
14. N-B7+	K-Q1
15. B-N5+	P-B3
16. BxP+	

Black is checkmated on the next move.

36. *Pirc Defense*

The thorny theme in this opening is the veiled threat of P-K5. Black fails to prepare a post for his king knight and so falls prey to a ferocious attack.

1. P-K4	P-KN3
2. P-Q4	B-N2
3. P-KB4	P-Q3
4. N-KB3	N-KB3

| 5. B-Q3 | 0-0 |
| 6. 0-0 | QN-Q2?! |

Just a slight error often prefaces an overwhelming attack. Black must ready a spot for his knight with either 6. . . . P-B3, or challenge White's center with 6. . . . P-B4.

| 7. P-K5! | N-K1 |

Ignominious retreat, but forced.

| 8. Q-K1 | P-QB4 |

Too slow and, incidentally, too late. Correct, even if awkward, is 8. . . . P-K3.

| 9. P-B5! | QPxP |
| 10. BPxP! | RPxP |

Ready to answer 11. PxKP with . . . NxP! 12. NxN Q-Q5+!

| 11. Q-R4! | KPxP |
| 12. B-R6 | . . . |

To eliminate the defender of the dark squares around the king.

| 12. . . . | N(1)-B3 |
| 13. N-N5! | . . . |

The accuracy of every move is vital in pursuing an initiative afforded by a relatively minor error.

| 13. . . . | N-K4? |

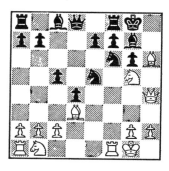

Black tires. The queen knight stood well defending his colleague. 13. ... P-N4 would have kept the battle going.

14. RxN!!   . . .

If 14. ... PxR, 15. BxB, or if 14. ... BxR, 15. B-N7, with mate in either case.

14. ...   **B-R1**

The rest is a demonstration of how to win a won game.

15. R-B1	**R-K1**
16. B-B8!!	**B-B3**
17. RxB!!	. . .

Imagine the effect of the queen rook, if that were brought up!

17. ...	**PxR**
17. Q-R6!	**RxB**
19. Q-R7	

Black has been checkmated.

37. *Pirc Defense*

Black appears to weaken his position, but actually he gains a tremendous preponderance in the center.

1. P-K4	**P-KN3**
2. P-Q4	**B-N2**
3. P-QB3	**P-Q4**

The use of an irregular move forces an opponent to think for himself. The simple 4. PxP gives White the better game.

4. Q-R4+?!	**B-Q2**
5. Q-N3	**PxP!**
6. QxP	**N-QB3**
7. Q-R6	**R-N1**
8. N-Q2	**N-B3**

N.B.: The capture of the queen knight pawn has resulted in a logjam of the White forces. There is no convenient way to develop without allowing Black to dissolve his double pawns, after which White's position becomes weak on the dark squares.

9. P-B3	PxP
10. KNxP	0-0
11. N-B4?!	. . .

Directly, 11. B-K2 followed by 12. 0-0 is correct.

11. . . .	N-Q4
12. B-Q2?!	. . .

There is no point in abandoning the defense of the queen knight pawn!

12. . . .	N-N3!
13. B-K2	NxN
14. BxN	RxP
15. B-N3	. . .

Apparently White relied on the text to ensconce the rook; however, he has not anticipated the ensuing break, ripping open the long dark diagonal. Surely he would have played 15. 0-0.

15. . . .	P-K4!
16. P-Q5	. . .

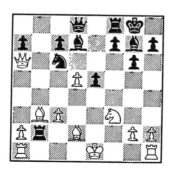

A futile attempt to close the king file.

16. . . .	N-N5!!
17. PxN	P-K5

18. B-N5	Q-K1!
19. N-Q2	P-K6
20. N-B3	B-B6+
21. K-Q1	RxNP
22. R-K1	B-N5
23. Q-B1	R-Q7+

And after 24. K-B1 B-N7+ 25. K-N1 Q-K5+, the party is over.

38. *Pirc Defense*

Adrift in uncharted waters, Black does not stay alert. He is awakened to find his ship of state boarded by a brigand queen whose word is final.

1. P-K4	P-KN3
2. P-Q4	B-N2
3. N-KB3	P-Q3
4. B-QB4	N-KB3
5. Q-K2	P-B4

Correct is P-B3 to answer P-K5 with the exchange of pawns and then the posting of the king knight at Q4.

6. P-K5!	QPxP
7. PxKP	N-Q4
8. 0-0	P-K3
9. R-Q1	0-0

No hurry to castle; better to protect the dark squares with P-KR3.

| 10. B-KN5! | Q-N3 |

Defense is actually offered by the awkward Q-Q2! Black decides it is easier to give up a pawn and be compensated by the possession of the two bishops. The easy path leads to disaster, for White will not grab the pawn, losing time for the attack.

| 11. BxN | PxB |
| 12. N-B3! | ... |

Rather than a pawn White looks toward those weak dark squares around the enemy king.

| 12. ... | P-Q5 |

Advisable was 12. ... B-K3 13. NxP BxN 14. RxB QxP 15. QR-Q1 N-B3 with good counter-play.

| 13. N-Q5 | Q-R3 |
| 14. Q-Q2! | ... |

Of course, the exchange of queens would not enhance the attack.

| 14. ... | B-N5 |

Black indirectly defends against N-B7 and the fork of his queen and rook: 15. N-B7 Q-B3 16. NxR BxN! 17. PxB N-Q2 and after capturing the cornered knight Black has enough for the exchange.

| 15. B-B6! | BxN?? |

Mortally neglecting development with N-Q2.

16. Q-R6!!

The diagram, with mate included, is worth a thousand words.

39. *Pirc Defense (By Transposition)*

An uninvited queen enters the foreign castle, leaving herself no line of retreat. Grateful for the visit, the enemy king puts the precious lady under house-arrest.

1. N-KB3	P-KN3
2. P-Q4	B-N2
3. P-K4	P-Q3
4. N-B3	N-QB3
5. P-KR3	. . .

More forceful is 5. P-Q5.

5. . . .	P-K4
6 P-Q5	. . .

Not consistent with move five; 6. B-K3 keeps the tension.

6. . . .	QN-K2
7. P-KN4	P-QB3!
8. B-K3	PxP
9. NxQP	NxN
10. QxN	N-B3
11. B-N5+	K-K2!

The king is just as safe in the center; and thus, with this *risky* move the initiative passes to Black.

12. Q-Q3	P-QR3
13. B-QB4	P-QN4
14. B-N3	B-N2
15. N-Q2	R-QB1
16. P-KB4	. . .

Indications of delusions of grandeur are apparent. Good defense required P-KB3 and K-B2.

16. . . .	N-Q2
17. Q-B1	R-B1
18. Q-B2	N-B4
19. Q-R4+	K-K1

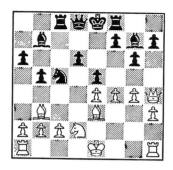

Why exchange queens, when a pawn is hanging?

20. QxRP??	NxB!
21. NxN	B-KB3

This is why: R-KR1 will win the queen.

40. Ruy Lopez (Bird Defense)

Once in a while the Bird Defense to the Ruy reappears. Sorry for the defense, it is the inveterate pawn-grabber who revives the debut.

1. P-K4	P-K4
2. N-KB3	N-QB3
3. B-N5	N-Q5

The idea of the opening is to gain time for development at slight cost to the pawn structure.

4. NxN	PxN
5. P-Q3	B-N5+

This move doesn't lose, but it does contradict the theme of the opening. Now it is Black who loses time while his bishop is jostled about.

6. P-B3	PxP
7. NxP!	. . .

The recapture, 7. PxP, adds more pawn power to the center, but bringing out the knight is more important here.

| 7 ... | Q-B3?! |

Minor pieces come out before major ones.

| 8. 0-0 | BxN |

Practically forced, since the knight is no longer pinned and N-Q5 was threatened.

| 9. PxB | QxBP?? |

The losing move. Time is far too precious. A reasonable plan was N-K2, P-B3, P-Q3 and 0-0.

| 10. R-N1 | Q-KB3 |
| 11. B-N2 | Q-KN3 |

If 11. ... Q-KR3, then 12. Q-B1 QxQ 13. KRxQ and White regains his pawn with advantage, e.g., P-QB3 14. BxNP PxB 15. BxR P-B3 16. RxP followed by R-KR5 freeing the cornered bishop. Therefore, Black must play 13. ... P-KB3, when White gets his rook on the seventh rank by RxP.

| 12. P-B4 | N-B3 |

"Always check it might be mate" is an untenable tenet: 12. ... Q-N3+ 13. K-R1 QxB 14. BxP!

| 13. P-B5 | Q-R3 |

Here's a trap: 13. ... Q-R4 14. R-B3! 0-0? 15. BxN PxB 16. R-N3+ winning the queen.

| 14. B-R3 | ... |

Preventing castles.

| 14. ... | P-R3 |
| 15. B-B4 | P-QN4 |

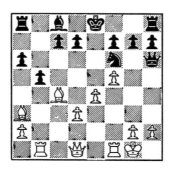

On 15. ... P-Q3, 16. P-K5! But anyway ...

16. P-K5!   **Q-K6+**

Black would like to rid himself of an annoying prelate, but 16. ... PxB 17. PxN leaves Black's king wide open to a mating attack.

17. K-R1   **N-K5**

He may as well, for 17. ... N-N1 18. BxP+ KxB 19. Q-R5+ P-N3 20. PxP double check leads to mate anyway. After the text, however, White may also win with 18. PxN PxB (or QxB) 19. Q-Q5 etc.

18. BxP+   **K-Q1**

Again 18. ... KxB is stymied by 19. Q-R5+!

19. B-B1!   **N-B7+**
20. RxN   **QxR**
21. B-N5

and Black is checkmated.

41. *Ruy Lopez*

The defender must keep the position closed. A faulty developing move (12. ... N-B3) and a temporary sacrifice (13. BxP!) smashes the game wide open.

1. P-K4	P-K4
2. N-KB3	N-QB3
3. B-N5	N-Q5
4. NxN	PxN
5. 0-0	P-QB3
6. B-R4	P-KN3
7. P-Q3	B-N2
8. B-B4	P-QR4

Application of the Noah's Ark Theme threatening to trap the bishop.

9. P-QR3	P-Q3
10. N-Q2	P-QN4
11. B-QN3	P-R5
12. B-R2	N-B3?

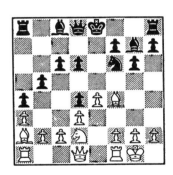

What would you play?

| 13. BxP! | QxB |
| 14. P-K5! | Q-K2 |

Naturally 14. .... QxKP loses the queen.

| 15. PxN | QxBP |
| 16. R-K1+ | K-B1 |

The loss of the castling privilege is frequently accompanied by deprivation of the services of the associated rook.

| 17. N-K4 | Q-K4?! |

Looking for more trouble; 17. . . . Q-Q1! is best.

| 18. Q-Q2 | P-R3? |

Try 18. . . . K-N1 and if 19. Q-N4, B-B1.

| 19. Q-N4+ | K-N1 |
| 20. N-Q6!! | P-QB4 |

If 20. . . . Q-R4, 21. NxBP!

21. RxQ	PxQ
22. BxP+	K-R2
23. RxNP	

White has too many pawns.

42. Ruy Lopez (Exchange Variation)

A lesson in capitalizing on an open king rook file. The pinning bishop sacrifices itself to facilitate the opening of that file. Under pressure it is often very difficult to refrain from accepting such a sacrifice.

1. P-K4	P-K4
2. N-KB3	N-QB3
3. B-N5	P-QR3
4. BxN	QPxB
5. 0-0	. . .

Practical Chess Openings dubs this move weak as Black can "safely reply with B-KN5(!)." If one argues the point, he should observe that Fischer has been unique in his success against that *safe* reply. On that basis alone, however, we could not recommend White's system, for there is only one Fischer. But let us consider the situation objectively. Immediately taking the bishop is surely weak: 5. 0-0 B-KN5!? 6. P-KR3 P-KR4! 7. P-Q3 (7. PxB?! PxP 8. NxP?? Q-R5 and mates.) Q-B3 8. PxB PxP 9. N-N5 Q-R3 10. N-KR3 Q-R5 11. K-R2 PxN 12. P-KN3 Q-R2 with a strong initiative for Black.

| 5. . . . | B-KN5!? |

After 5. ... P-B3 6. P-Q4 B-KN5 7. P-B3 Q-Q2, the position is unclear. The better or, rather, the more alert player must win, especially since most positions must be deemed unclear.

6. P-KR3	P-KR4!
7. P-B3	. . .

Unclear is 7. P-Q3 Q-B3 8. QN-Q2 P-KN4!?

7. ...	B-QB4
8. P-Q4	PxP

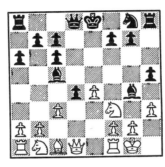

White had his eye on the bishop, now he lays hands on him. Correct is 9. P-K5. Black has been given a free hand.

9. PxB?	RPxP
10. N-N5	Q-Q3!

Forcing P-K5 after which Black, if need be, may occupy K5 with the queen without fear of R-K1. The White pawn is also more vulnerable farther advanced.

11. P-K5	Q-R3
12. N-KR3	Q-N3
13. N-N5	. . .

13. N-B4 Q-R2(!) offers no relief.

13. ...	Q-R4
14. N-R3	0-0-0
15. P-QB4	. . .

Only temporarily shutting out Black's bishop.

15. ...   PxN

Black has regained his piece and won two pawns.

43. *Ruy Lopez (Exchange Variation)*

1. P-K4	P-K4
2. N-KB3	N-QB3
3. B-N5	P-QR3
4. BxN	QPxB
5. 0-0	B-KN5!?
6. P-KR3	P-KR4!
7. P-Q3	...

Obviously not 7. P-Q4 BxN!

7. ...	Q-B3
8. QN-Q2	N-K2
9. P-QN4?	...

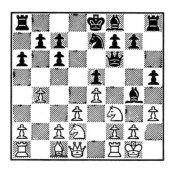

The text prepares for PxB, but now is the time! Let's look:
9. PxB PxP 10. R-K1 Q-R3?! 11. K-B1 PxN 12. QxP with a
satisfactory game. If 11. ... Q-R8+, 12. N-N1! R-R7 13. QxP!
White was worried about ... B-QB4, but that cannot come
until much later.

9. ...	N-N3
10. PxB?	...

Although 10. Q-K1 is better, frankly, there is no real solution to the impending N-B5 and BxRP(!).

10. ...	PxP
11. P-N3	N-B5!

On 12. PxN, Q-R3 decides, but some hope is offered by 12. R-K1, providing an escape hatch for the king.

12. N-R4?	RxN!!
13. PxR	QxP

On 14. N-B4, P-N6; so ...

14. N-B3	Q-R6

After 15. BxN PxN White must give up the queen.

15. N-K1	BxP!
16. BxN	PxB
17. Q-B1	0-0-0!!

Yes, 17. ... BxN wins a piece owing to the mating threat of P-B6, but the text guarantees mate.

18. QxP	R-R1
19. Q-B5+	K-N1

And White gives up his ghost.

44. *Ruy Lopez* (*Exchange Variation*)

Fischer favors this opening. Why not whip up something for some one who might play Fischer's moves—to a point! If you can convince your opponent you are quaking in your boots and dying for the half point, he may blindly rush into the trap.

1. P-K4	P-K4
2. N-KB3	N-QB3
3. B-N5	P-QR3
4. BxN	QPxB
5. 0-0	B-KN5
6. P-KR3	P-KR4!

The bishop for the present is immune, for the opening of the rook file would herald checkmate. Black may therefore maintain the pin.

7. P-B3   ...

White intends to release the pin with Q-N3. He may also decide to gain the initiative by sacrificing a pawn: 8. P-Q4 PxP 9. PxP BxN 10. QxB (PxB is also good.) QxP 11. R-Q1.

7. ...   **Q-Q6!!**

In anticipation of 8. Q-N3 BxN 9. QxP R-Q1 10. QxP+ R-Q2 11. PxB R-R3!! and Black wins.

8. PxB?   ...

If White plays to win, he should play R-K1. With the text he only thinks he is playing for the win.

8. ...   **PxP**
9. NxP   ...

A big improvement is N-N5! Now the kettle begins to boil.

9. ...   **B-Q3!**

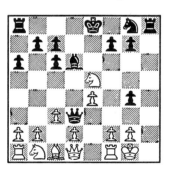

White should now allow Black to draw by perpetual check: 10. NxQ B-R7+ 11. K-R1 B-N6+ 12. K-N1 B-R7+ etc. They say that more often than not, Black should be satisfied with a draw anyway!

10. NxNP?	N-B3!!
11. NxN+	PxN
12. Q-N4??	. . .

Apparently White is now willing to draw, for he decides to permit B-R7+. 12. P-K5 was the last chance.

| 12. . . . | R-R8+!! |
| 13. KxR | QxR Checkmate!! |

45. *Ruy Lopez* (*Marshall Attack*)

Black ignores an old recommendation which gives him good play for the pawn. White then invites his opponent to fork his rook and bishop. Black should have attended to his other commitments.

1. P-K4	P-K4
2. N-KB3	N-QB3
3. B-N5	P-QR3
4. B-R4	N-B3
5. 0-0	B-K2
6. R-K1	P-QN4
7. B-N3	0-0
8. P-B3	P-Q4
9. PxP	NxP
10. NxP	NxN
11. RxN	P-QB3
12. P-Q4	B-Q3
13. R-K1	Q-R5
14. P-KN3	Q-R6
15. R-K4?!	. . .

This move has been abandoned by the expert because of the reply 15. . . . P-KN4 preventing 16. R-R4. For if 16. BxP, Q-B4 wins. Current theory is 15. B-K3 B-N5 16. Q-Q3.

15. . . .	N-B3?!
16. R-R4	Q-B4
17. B-KB4	. . .

No doubt 17. B-B2 should have been considered.

17. ...   R-Q1

There exists the possibility of 17. ... P-N4 18. BxB PxR
19. BxR KxB 20. B-B2 and White has the edge.

18. N-Q2   ...

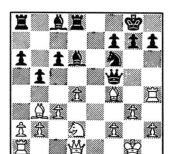

"Now's the chance for the kill," thinks Black.

18. ...   P-N4??

Aware that he stands worse, Black confronts White with the
possibility of material loss hoping to force a repetition of
moves, 19. B-B2 Q-Q4 20. B-N3 Q-KB4 21. B-B2 etc.

19. B-B2   Q-Q4
20. N-K4!   ...

A totally unexpected surprise. The rest is forced.

20. ...   NxN
21. BxN   QxB
22. BxP   Q-K1
23. BxR   QxB
24. Q-R5   K-B1
25. R-K1   B-K3
26. QxRP   K-K1
27. R(4)-K4   B-K2
28. P-KB4!!

The pin on the king file decides.

46. *Ruy Lopez (Marshall Attack)*

One trap leads to another. Black catches White, but he omits a simple finesse and it is he himself who is snared.

1. P-K4	P-K4
2. N-KB3	N-QB3
3. B-N5	P-QR3
4. B-R4	N-B3
5. 0-0	B-K2
6. R-K1	P-QN4
7. B-N3	0-0
8. P-B3	P-Q4
9. PxP	NxP
10. NxP	NxN
11. RxN	N-B3
12. P-Q4	B-Q3
13. R-K1	N-N5
14. P-KR3	Q-R5!
15. Q-B3!	. . .

After 15. PxN White encounters the lethal . . . BxP 16. P-B3 (If the queen moves, then Q-R7+ followed by Q-R8 mate.) B-N6 17. PxB Q-R7+ 18. K-B1 Q-R8+ 19. K-K2 QR-K1+ 20. B-K3 BxR and White won't see daylight.

15. . . .	NxP!
16. QxN?	. . .

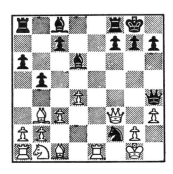

Correct is 16. R-K2.

16. . . .   B-N6??

After 16. . . . B-R7+ 17. K-B1 B-N6! Black has an excellent game.

17. QxP+!!   RxQ

Without check, and that's the difference.

18. R-K8

Checkmate, for the rook that might have interposed is pinned.

47. *Ruy Lopez*

Black gives up a piece for a speculative attack. If the defender plays 12. B-K3. Black picks up two more pawns: 12. . . . QxRP+ 13. K-B1 Q-R8+ 14. K-K2 QxP with more to follow. Faced with such an unsavory prospect, White prefers the easier way and consequently walks into a rare variant of *smothered mate*. Even with the *more to follow* White should have been glad to be alive.

1. P-K4	P-K4
2. N-KB3	N-QB3
3. B-N5	P-QR3
4. B-R4	N-B3
5. 0-0	P-QN4
6. B-N3	B-N2
7. R-K1	B-B4
8. P-B3	. . .

Intending to build a pawn center with gain of tempo on Black's king bishop. A fine idea if correctly implemented.

8. . . .   N-KN5?!

Black ought to play B-N3 and P-Q3.

9. P-Q4!	PxP
10. PxP?	. . .

The knight must first be ousted with P-KR3.

10. . .	QNxP!!
11. NxN	Q-R5
12. N-KB3?	. . .

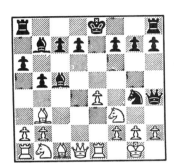

More than one mistake is necessary but there it is!

White should play B-K3 as suggested above. He expects 12. ... BxP+ 13. K-B1 NxP+ 14. NxN BxR 15. QxB QxN 16. N-B3 with two pieces for a rook. But here comes the shocker.

12. ...	QxBP+!
13. K-R1	Q-N8+!!
14. N(or R)xQ	N-B7

Checkmate!!

48. *Ruy Lopez*

Punishment was never so swift for the proverbial pawn-grabber. Who could ever anticipate White's thirteenth move?

1. P-K4	P-K4
2. N-KB3	N-QB3
3. B-N5	P-QR3
4. B-R4	N-B3
5. 0-0	P-QN4
6. B-N3	B-B4

Black's last is rarely seen these days. Nevertheless, it's not bad.

7. P-B3	NxP?

In this and similar positions B-N3 and P-Q3 is to be recommended. The method of retribution is not obvious. Observe!

8. Q-K2	P-Q4
9. P-Q3!	...

Gaining time to clear the king file.

9. ...	N-B3
10. P-Q4	B-K2

Black is completely disorganized, having lost time with the pawn-grab.

11. PxP	N-K5
12. R-Q1	B-K3
13. P-B4!	..

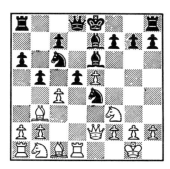

If Black could ignore the move, he would be all right. Unfortunately, his queen pawn is under siege.

13. ...	NPxP

Otherwise PxQP winning a piece.

14. B-R4!!

After either 14. ... Q-Q2 15. N-Q4 or 14. ... B-Q2 15. RxP White wins a piece!

49. Ruy Lopez

A game can end abruptly and very early. If the nerves in the hand that moves the pieces are not hooked up with those of the brain, there is wood pushing but no Chess. Black has a chance to plan his game. Instead he blindly recalls the maxim *the bishop is better than the knight* and *saves* his king bishop. He asks no further questions.

1.	P-K4	P-K4
2.	N-KB3	N-QB3
3.	B-N5	P-QR3
4.	B-R4	N-B3
5.	0-0	P-QN4
6.	B-N3	B-B4
7.	NxP!	. . .

A common sacrificial motif. In regaining his piece White hopes to gain control of the center with pawns since Black's central pawn has been removed.

7.	. . .	NxN
8.	P-Q4	B-N3??

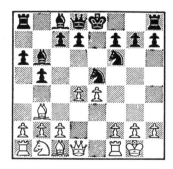

Terrible! May we suggest: 8. . . . . B-N2 9. PxN NxP 10. B-Q5 Q-N1! 11. BxB QxB 12. Q-N4 0-0-0! Or: 9. PxB Q-K2 10. N-B3 0-0-0.

9.	PxN	N-N1
10.	Q-Q5	Resigns.

The threats of QxR and QxP mate cannot simultaneously be parried. If one plays tournament Chess, winning a game like this will provide a well-deserved rest day.

50. *Ruy Lopez*

A close friend and former champion of Rome, Italy, Doctor Anthony A. Blasi inquired of me as to a reasonable method of meeting the Worrall Attack (6. Q-K2). Tony always disdained the draw, a win for him being the only reasonable outcome of any game! Of course, this request is tantamount to demanding that one's doctor produce a cure for the common cold. But with all this, one thing has been ascertained: doctors, and Chess masters, too, consult! I advised, "Play Chess!" What else could I say, "Take an aspirin?"

1.	P-K4	P-K4
2.	N-KB3	N-QB3
3.	B-N5	P-QR3
4.	B-R4	N-B3
5.	0-0	B-K2
6.	Q-K2	. . .

This move unfolds a double purpose. (1) To bolster the center with P-QB3 and P-Q4 by stationing the king rook on Q1 where it occupies the same file as the Black queen. (2) To avoid the Marshall Attack, if possible, by responding to Black's future P-Q4 with P-Q3, a solid move the idea of which is a slow but sure buildup on the king side.

6.	. . .	P-QN4
7.	B-N3	0-0
8.	P-B3	P-Q4

Since the queen is already on K2, White may conveniently play 9. P-Q3 without fear of a disruptive queen swap.

| 9. | PxP?! | P-K5 |

This pawn reaches K5 in an obscure variation of the Marshall Attack in which the White queen would be developed much later and the White rook stationed on K1—a time-saving configuration, if one is to permit . . . P-K5.

    10. N-N5   . . .

Another try is 10. PxN PxN 11. QxP B-KN5 12. Q-N3 B-Q3 13. P-KB4 with unclear play.

    10. . . .   **N-K4**

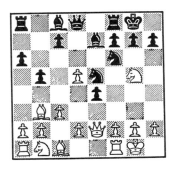

Development versus material: the eternal controversy.

    11. NxKP?   . . .

Correct is P-Q4!

    11. . . .   **NxN**
    12. QxN   **B-Q3**
    13. P-Q4   . . .

Now 13. P-KB4 is required.

    13. . . .   **P-KB4!**
    14. Q-K1   **N-B6+!!**
    15. PxN   **Q-R5**
    16. Q-K6+   . . .

After 16. P-KB4, R-B3 decides.

    16. . . .   **BxQ**

To avoid immediate mate White drops his queen.

51. *Ruy Lopez*

The Noah's Ark Trap is one of the oldest in the business. The method: to gain time by prodding vulnerable pieces with an advancing pawn phalanx which gradually corners an over-extended bishop. Black has the idea. White knows this and so the old ark never gets afloat.

1. P-K4	P-K4
2. N-KB3	N-QB3
3. B-N5	P-QR3
4. B-R4	P-QN4

With this somewhat premature move half the ark is built.

5. B-N3	N-R4
6. 0-0	. . .

Not as sharp as 6. P-Q4 but better than 6. NxP Q-K2 7. P-Q4 P-Q3 8. N-B3 QxP+ 9. B-K3 B-Q2 with equality; but not 9. ... B-N2? 10. 0-0 N-KB3 11. R-K1 B-K2 12. P-B4! and White has a big edge, R. Byrne-Lombardy, Seattle, 1965.

6. ...	P-Q3
7. P-Q4	PxP

White is slightly better after 7. ... NxB 8. RPxN P-KB3 9. P-B4.

8. NxP	NxB

White could have played 8. QxP, and if then Black should float the Old Noah's Ark, he's beaten back by a bitter wind: 8. ... P-QB4? 9. BxP+! KxB 10. Q-Q5+ B-K3 11. N-N5+! We suggest that after White's text Black should continue: 8. ... B-N2 9. B-Q2 NxB 10. RPxN P-N3 11. P-QB4 P-QB4! with an active game.

9. RPxN	B-N2

The big difference is that White need not waste time with B-Q2 and may proceed with the attack.

| 10. R-K1! | N-K2 |

A careless 10. . . . N-B3 allows 11. P-K5!

| 11. N-QB3 | Q-Q2 |
| 12. N-Q5 | P-QB4 |

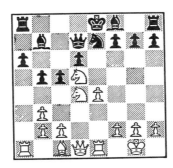

Making the best of bankruptcy.

| 13. N-N6 | Q-Q1 |
| 14. N-B5!! | . . . |

White doesn't fall for 14. NxR PxN, winning two pieces for a rook.

| 14. . . . | NxN |

The queen pawn must be defended.

15. PxN+	B-K2
16. NxR	QxN
17. QxP	Q-Q1
18. B-B4	. . .

Black is the exchange down and still cannot even castle.

52. *Ruy Lopez (Schliemann Defense)*

Black can get snared either way: to take or not to take the knight, that is the question.

1. P-K4	P-K4
2. N-KB3	N-QB3
3. B-N5	P-QR3
4. B-R4	P-B4
5. N-B3!?	...

Other, and more common alternatives are PxP, the solid P-Q3, and BxN. Introduced in Lombardy vs. Sherwin, US Championship, 1958, the novel text is quite sharp and seems to maintain the edge that theory attributes to White in this opening.

5. ...	P-QN4
6. B-N3	P-N5?!

The idea is difficult to fathom and so Black bites for the pawn. N-B3 is playable. Bisguier suggests: 6. ... PxP! 7. NxP(4) P-Q4 8. N-B3 N-B3 9. P-Q4 PxP 10. NxP(4) NxN 11. QxN P-B3 with equality. This seems to be Black's best and only continuation, although one might further examine the possibilities inherent in 7. KNxP, prior to accepting the analysis.

7. N-Q5	PxP
8. P-Q4!!	...

Now the trap may take two entirely different roads.

(1) To take the piece.

| 8. . . . | PxN |
| 9. QxP | NxP? |

Also bad, but far better than the text is 9. . . . B-K2 10. NxP+ QxN 11. Q-B7+ K-Q1 12. QxNP N-B3 13. QxR+ N-K1 14. B-B7! Q-Q3 15. QxN+ K-B2 and Black has some compensation for his material deficit.

| 10. Q-R5+ | P-N3 |
| 11. QxKP+ | B-K2 |

If 11. . . . N-K2, 12. N-B6 mate.

12. QxR	NxB
13. QxN+	B-B1
14. B-R6!	. . .

White wins scads of material.

(2) Or not to take the piece.

| 8. . . . | PxP? |

In the King's Gambit there is an offshoot line called the Muzio Gambit in which White gives up the king knight in a similar position. Superior development and a ferocious attack more than compensate for the sacrificed material, especially in over-the-board play. Aware of the Muzio, and observing the similarities here, Black prefers to decline the piece. He may as well be hanged for a wolf as for a lamb!

9. NxP	N-B3
10. B-N5	B-K2
11. N-B5!	P-N3
12. N(B)xB	KNxN
13. QxN	R-B1

After 13. . . . NxN, 14. Q-B7 mate.

| 14. NxN | . . . |

Black loses the queen and mate follows.

53. *Ruy Lopez (Schliemann Defense)*

En Passant is a privilege, not a necessity!

1. P-K4	P-K4
2. N-KB3	N-QB3
3. B-N5	P-B4
4. N-B3	PxP
5. QNxP	P-Q4
6. NxP	PxN
7. NxN	Q-Q4

To force White to defend the bishop and thus hinder His Grace with one of his own pawns. A weaker defense in a well-worn line is 8. ... PxN 9. BxP+ B-Q2 10. Q-R5+ K-K2 11. Q-K5+ B-K3 12. P-KB4 N-R3 13. QxP R-QN1 14. P-Q4 K-B2 15. P-B5 NxP 16. 0-0! with powerful pressure for White.

8. P-QB4	Q-Q3
9. P-B5!?	...

Slightly better is NxP discovered check, but White wishes to unblock his king bishop and also lure the Black queen away from her king.

9. ...	QxBP
10. Q-R4	N-B3
11. P-Q4!	PxPe.p.??

The queen should return to Q3 where she again protects the king. The king pawn still remains to block the king file.

12. 0-0	PxN
13. BxP+	B-Q2

The pin prevents White from taking the rook, but strangely, he's not after the rook—yet!

14. BxB+!	K-Q1

After 14. ... NxB 15. Q-K4+ does win the rook!

15. B-B6	R-QN1
16. B-K3	Q-N5
17. Q-R6!	QxP
18. QxP+	. . .

There is no point in continuing for after 18. ... B-Q3, 19. QR-N1 wins at least a rook.

54. *Ruy Lopez* (*Schliemann Defense*)

Again *En Passant*—abusing the privilege!

1. P-K4	P-K4
2. N-KB3	N-QB3
3. B-N5	P-B4
4. N-B3	PxP
5. QNxP	P-Q4
6. N-N3	P-K5
7. N-K5	. . .

Another good idea is N-Q4, followed by P-Q3, undermining Black's pawn center.

7. ...	Q-Q3
8. BxN+	. . .

Satisfactory in varying degrees are NxN and P-KB4.

8. ...	PxB
9. P-Q4	PxPe.p.?

Abusing the e.p. privilege. Much better is 9. ... N-B3, followed by P-B4.

10. 0-0!	PxP
11. QxBP	N-K2
12. R-K1	B-Q2?!

Because of the pin on the king file the bishop pawn hangs; nevertheless B-K3 defends more efficiently.

| 13. B-N5 | B-K3! |

Ironic, isn't it?

14. R-K2	0-0-0
15. Q-R4	K-N2
16. N-Q3!	B-Q2

White threatened to win by 17. B-B4 Q-Q2 18. N-B5+!

17. B-B4	Q-B3
18. N-B5+	K-R1
19. BxP	. . .

When the hapless rook runs away, the queen bishop hangs—besides, there is the mating threat of B-N6!

55. Ruy Lopez (*Schliemann Defense*)

Who wouldn't offer a pawn in return for a mating attack?

1.	P-K4	P-K4
2.	N-KB3	N-QB3
3.	B-N5	P-B4
4.	N-B3	N-Q5?!

Violates the principle of moving a piece twice in the early stages of the opening, but, because of its novelty, keeps the opponent off balance. The older moves are more steady, e.g., PxP or N-B3; but then theory has consistently held this opening under suspicion anyway!

5.	B-R4	. . .

Theory runs: 5. NxP Q-N4 6. 0-0 PxP 7. P-B4 PxPe.p. 8. NxBP Q-QB4 with a lively game and chances for both sides.

5.	. . .	N-KB3
6.	PxP	. . .

Or the more solid 6. P-Q3.

6.	. . .	B-B4
7.	0-0	0-0
8.	NxP?	. . .

On move five, fine, but not here when Black, having completed his development, is able to take immediate action.

8. ...	P-Q4
9. N-B3	BxP
10. NxN	BxN
11. P-Q3	N-N5
12. B-B4	NxBP!!

There was no time for White to maneuver his bishop to KN3 to defend the king bishop pawn.

| 13. RxN | BxR+ |
| 14. KxB | Q-R5+ |

White has two pieces for a rook, but sadly, the pieces are useless. Observe the fellow on QR4.

15. B-N3	Q-Q5+
16. K-K1	B-N5
17. Q-B1	P-B3!

And with the threat of QR-K1+ Black coasts to victory.

56. *Ruy Lopez*

The trap that arises after 14. ... N-B3(?) seems too convenient. All White does to induce Black's fall is play *good moves*. But then, that's the problem for all of us!

1. P-K4	P-K4
2. N-KB3	N-QB3
3. B-N5	P-QR3
4. B-R4	P-Q3
5. 0-0	B-Q2
6. P-Q4	N-B3
7. P-B3	B-K2
8. QN-Q2	0-0
9. R-K1	...

Not Q-K2 which is answered by NxQP! winning a pawn.

| 9. ... | P-QN4 |
| 10. B-N3 | PxP?! |

More active is B-N5.

11. PxP	N-QN5?!

Far too ambitious for a man with a cramped game; 11. ...
B-N5 still may be played.

12. P-K5!	N-K1

Not possible is: 12. ... PxP 13. PxP N(3)-Q4 14. P-QR3.

13. N-K4	PxP
14. NxP	N-KB3?

The temptation to redeploy this piece on its native soil was
too great. Correct was N-Q3.

15. NxN+	PxN

There is no choice: 15. ... BxN 16. NxP! RxN 17. BxR+
KxB 18. Q-N3+ and White remains with the exchange ahead.

16. NxB	QxN
17. B-R6!	KR-K1?

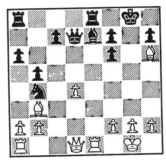

If one desires to fight on, one must sometimes surrender
material. In this case Black should give up the Ox—that is,
a rook for a minor piece.

18. RxB!	RxR

If 18. ... QxR, 19. Q-N4+ and mate.

19. Q-B3!

The double threat of QxR and Q-N3+ followed by mate cannot be handled.

57. *Ruy Lopez*

The trap that's there but isn't. Hallucination, or taking an opponent's word that a trap is there when it is not, are a player's worst enemies. Psychology is the most precipitous stratagem. White falls for it; either that or he plays for the win right in the face of a fatal mating attack.

1. P-K4	P-K4
2. N-KB3	N-QB3
3. B-N5	P-QR3
4. B-R4	P-Q3
5. 0-0	B-Q2
6. P-B3	KN-K2

The normal continuation is: 6. ... N-B3 7. P-Q4 B-K2 8. R-K1 0-0, but that's another game.

7. P-Q4	N-N3
8. R-K1	B-K2
9. QN-Q2	0-0
10. N-B1	. . .

It is reasonable to avoid the pin with P-KR3.

10. ...	B-N5!
11. P-Q5	. . .

There is opinion abroad that the impending sacrifice is made even stronger by the text. Apparently, 20 years ago there was a game in which White, unaware of the danger, played BxN and succumbed to the sacrifice. The point is that the trap works either way. The difference being that after 11. BxN Black wins, but after 11. P-Q5, played here, he can only force a draw!

11. ...	N-R5!

Retreating N-QN1 only permits White to organize after chasing the bishop with P-KR3. The text does not allow this owing to the rejoinder BxN, forcing PxB and thus the destruction of White's pawns.

12. PxN!   . . .

White can also safely decline the sacrifice: 12. N(1)-Q2 N-N1 13. P-KR3 B-R4 14. P-KN4!

12. . . .   **BxN!**

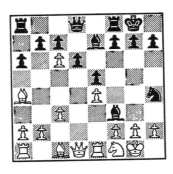

The trap begins!

13. Q-Q3??   . . .

Tantamount to resignation. Correct is 13. PxB Q-B1 14. PxP! Q-R6 15. N-K3 QR-N1 16. K-R1! NxP 17. N-B1 N-R5 18. N-K3 and a draw is forced by repetition of moves. After 15. . . . B-N4 16. B-Q7! NxP+ 17. QxN QxQ 18. PxR=Q and White has too much for the queen.

Had White essayed 11. BxN, he would not have had the threat on Black's queen rook nor the resource 16. B-Q7(!), as above, when he would most need it. Let us look again at the value of the move: 15. . . . B-N4 16. *B-Q7!* P-KB4 17. B-K6+ K-R1 18. PxR=Q RxQ 19. BxP and wins! Notice too that 15. . . . NxP+ 16. QxN and 17. PxR concedes too much for the queen.

13. . . .   **BxNP**
14. R-K3   **P-B4**

15. PxNP	R-N1
16. PxP	BxP
17. B-N3+	K-R1
18. B-K6	Q-K1!

White must play 19. B-Q5, after which he loses a vital pawn and thus the game.

58. *Scotch Opening*

Winning two pieces for a rook ordinarily is enough. Not so, says White, whose centralized rooks are poised to win the day. Suddenly Black casts a hypnotic spell over his rival and White drives him where he wants to go.

1. P-K4	P-K4
2. N-KB3	N-QB3
3. P-Q4	PxP
4. NxP	N-B3
5. NxN	NPxN
6. P-K5	N-Q4
7. N-Q2	. . .

Or 7. P-QB4.

| 7. . . . | Q-R5 |

Or simply 7. . . . P-Q3.

| 8. B-Q3 | N-N5 |
| 9. B-K4 | B-R3?! |

If one looks a move ahead, one perceives that such a move badly misplaces that piece, for White is able to bottleneck the bishop with his very next move.

| 10. P-B4 | P-KB4 |
| 11. BxKBP | . . . |

If prepared to meet P-Q4(!), then capture *en passant*.

| 11. . . . | B-B4? |

Black offered his KB pawn to open the file for a decisive attack. He did not foresee the coming shot!

| 12. BxP+! | K-K2 |

Naturally 12. .... KxB loses the queen to N-B3+!

13. 0-0	QR-KB1
14. N-B3!	RxN
15. QxR	KxB
16. Q-B5+	K-K1

Right to the point is 17. R-Q1, which prevents R-KB1 because of Q-Q7 mate. Then, B-N5 becomes a genuine threat.

| 17. B-N5? | ... |

White acts too quickly. But all is not lost; one more lemon is required!

17. ...	QxP
18. QR-B1	R-KB1
19. Q-R3?	...

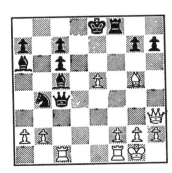

And there's the blunder. 19. B-B6 actually maintains some initiative for the material deficit.

| 19. ... | RxP!! |
| 20. RxQ | R-B6+! |

If 21. RxB, RxR checkmate!

59. *Scotch Opening*

Careless, unplanned development—and the fork does the trick.

1. P-K4	P-K4
2. N-KB3	N-QB3
3. P-Q4	PxP
4. NxP	B-B4

Much sharper than 4. . . . N-B3 5. NxN NPxN 6. B-Q3 which is known to favor White.

5. B-K3	Q-B3

Fischer's research into the archives brought to light 5. . . . Q-R5 which he analyzed and recommended as offering chances equal to those of any of the other choices.

6. P-QB3	Q-N3
7. N-Q2	. . .

So far, according to Hoyle. 7. . . . KN-K2 or B-N3 are both acceptable at this juncture. But one does not always follow the *book*, sometimes to one's great regret.

7. . . .	N-B3?!

Playable, if one has the right plan.

8. Q-B2	. . .

Defending the king pawn and preparing to castle long. White may then take advantage of his advantage in space to launch his king side attack.

8. . . .	0-0??

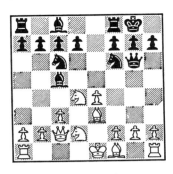

That old rule about castling again!

9. NxN!!

If 9. ... PxN, 10. BxB wins a piece; if 9. ... BxB(?), 10. N-K7+ forks the king and queen.

60. *Sicilian Defense*

Among the major problems for the defender in the Sicilian is the prevention of P-K5 and the ensuing attack on his king. If he solves this problem, then the extra central pawn, the characteristic of this defense, will stand him in good stead for the remainder of the game. But one careless developing move and the trap closes.

1. P-K4	P-QB4
2. N-KB3	P-Q3
3. P-Q4	PxP
4. NxP	N-KB3
5. N-QB3	P-QR3
6. B-N5	P-K3

Not 6. ... P-K4 7. N-B5 and White occupies the white squares, gaining a powerful grip on the position.

7. P-B4	QN-Q2

Fischer, the modern authority on either side of this opening, has recommended Q-N3.

| 8. Q-B3 | Q-B2 |
| 9. 0-0-0 | P-N4? |

Premature. White must seek out other traps after B-K2.

10. P-K5	B-N2
11. Q-R3	PxP
12. NxKP!	...

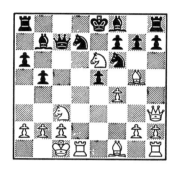

Strange that a relatively minor error can take all the starch out of a game. Black's ninth move returns to haunt him.

| 12. ... | PxN |
| 13. QxP+ | B-K2 |

There is 13. ... K-Q1 14. BxN+ PxB 15. QxP+, and that's all there is!

| 14. BxN | NxB |
| 15. BxP+ | K-B1 |

There is also 15. ... PxB 16. NxP Q-B3 17. N-Q6+ K-Q1 18. NxB+ etc.

| 16. PxP | B-R6 |
| 17. PxN | |

Black's only compensation for his lost game is the privilege of resigning.

61. Sicilian Defense

The square Q5, since the game Matanović versus Tal, Portorož, 1958, has been Black's biggest headache.

1. P-K4	P-QB4
2. N-KB3	P-Q3
3. P-Q4	PxP
4. NxP	N-KB3
5. N-QB3	P-QR3
6. B-N5	P-K3
7. P-B4	QN-Q2
8. Q-B3	Q-B2
9. 0-0-0	R-QN1?

Useless; B-K2 is necessary and good.

10. B-Q3	P-N4?

Compounding the error; B-K2 still offers defensive chances.

11. KR-K1	P-N5

Oh no! Perhaps P-R3 and P-N4, sacrificing a pawn is of some help. Now 11. .... B-K2 is refuted: 12. P-K5 P-N5 13. PxN PxP 14. NxP PxN 15. Q-R5+ P-N3 16. BxP+ PxB 17. QxP+ K-any 18. PxB mate.

12. N-Q5!	Q-N2

After 12. ... PxN 13. PxP+ B-K2 14. N-B6 and White wins scads of material.

13. BxP!

This is too much to endure; White surely has no trouble winning.

62. *Sicilian Defense*

The central pawn mass usually performs a holding action, depriving the White knights of vital attacking squares. When the pawns fail in this function, they become a pawn mess! Here White neatly explodes the pawn mess by undermining Black's light squares.

1. P-K4		P-QB4
2. N-KB3		P-Q3
3. P-Q4		PxP
4. NxP		N-KB3
5. N-QB3		P-QR3
6. B-N5		P-K3
7. P-B4		Q-B2

The aggressive idea of P-K5 must be anticipated.

8. Q-B3		P-QN4
9. 0-0-0		B-N2?!

Development of the queen knight to Q2 prevents the pawn-doubling.

10. BxN!		PxB
11. Q-R5!		. . .

This not only preys on the weak king bishop pawn but also blocks the king rook pawn, thereby restricting Black's king bishop. The threat is NxP.

11. ...		Q-B4
12. P-B5		K-K2

Necessary to break the pin on the king bishop pawn, but the text further limits the king bishop.

| 13. Q-R3 | N-B3 |

After 13. ... P-K4, Black leaves a gaping hole on his Q4.

| 14. NxN+ | BxN |
| 15. PxP | PxP |

The exchange of pawns has opened up paths to the Black king, which now stands helpless in the center.

| 16. B-Q3 | P-N5? |

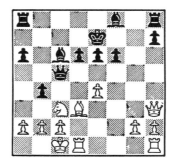

In a difficult position Black gets impatient, driving the knight where it wants to go. Correct was 16. ... P-KR4, intending either B-R3 or R-R3, depending on the future requirements of the position.

| 17. N-K2 | P-KR4 |
| 18. N-B4 |

Black cannot meet both QxP+ and N-N6+, either of which wins easily.

63. *Sicilian Defense*

Never take the queen knight pawn! This principle, expounded for over a century, can only be violated by a Fischer, who makes the pawn-grab the rule rather than the exception. Here a Fischer fan would emulate the supermaster. The maze of complications soon swallows the would-be master.

1. P-K4	P-QB4
2. N-KB3	P-Q3
3. P-Q4	PxP
4. NxP	N-KB3
5. N-QB3	P-QR3
6. B-N5	P-K3
7. P-B4	Q-N3

White sacs the queen knight pawn for the following reasons. First, moves such as R-QN1 and Q-B1 are too awkward. Second, 8. N-N3 allows ... Q-K6+, which equalizes easily. Finally, he hopes Black will not take the pawn!

8. Q-Q2	QxP
9. R-QN1	Q-R6
10. P-B5	N-B3
11. PxP	PxP
12. NxN	PxN
13. P-K5!	...

The pawn gives his life to breach the enemy pawn barrier.

13. ...	PxP
14. BxN	PxB
15. N-K4	B-K2

To be considered was 15. ... Q-K2!

16. B-K2	P-KR4
17. P-B4	P-KB4
18. R-N3	Q-R5

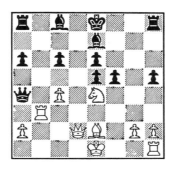

Now that the Black queen is safely tucked away, White can punish the pawn-grabber.

| 19. 0-0!! | PxN |
| 20. Q-Q1! | B-B4+ |

Black tries to prevent mate by blocking the queen file.

21. K-R1	B-Q5
22. BxP+	K-Q1
23. R-B7	QxRP
24. Q-KB1	Q-R8
25. R-N1	QxR
26. QxQ	RxB
27. Q-N4	P-B4
28. Q-N6+	

With the reproof, "Never take the queen knight pawn!"

64. *Sicilian Defense*

Driving away an enemy piece with a pawn very often emits the illusion of gain-of-time. But remember, a pawn play is permanent, for the infantry does not move backwards. A pawn move leaves behind weakness that can be repaired only by more valuable pieces, pieces that have more important tasks to accomplish. Here there is no such piece available for the job.

1. P-K4	P-QB4
2. N-KB3	P-Q3
3. P-Q4	PxP
4. NxP	N-KB3
5. N-QB3	P-QR3
6. B-N5	P-K3
7. Q-B3	QN-Q2
8. 0-0-0	Q-B2
9. Q-N3	P-QN4
10. B-Q3	B-N2

Better is 10. . . . P-N5.

| **11. KR-K1** | **P-R3?** |

Black has survived the early stages of the opening. He should now have played 11. ... B-K2 and then 12. ... P-R3, if necessary. 11. . . . P-N5 is met with 12. N-Q5(!).

| **12. BxN!** | **NxB?** |

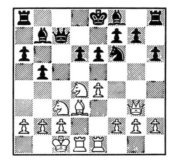

Unappetizing in appearance but quite safe was 12. . . . PxB, restraining the central advance P-K5.

| **13. P-K5!** | **PxP** |

If 13. ... N-Q2, then 14. PxP BxP (14. ... QxP 15. NxKP anyway!) 15. NxKP! PxN (15. ... BxQ 16. NxQ double discovered check!) 16. RxP+ and White wins.

| **14. N(3)xNP** | **Q-N3** |

A pretty mate ensues after 14. ... RPxN 15. BxP+ K-Q2 16. N-B5+ PxN 17. QxP+ QxQ 18. RxP mate. Or 15. ... N-Q2 16. NxP! PxN 17. RxN QxR 18. Q-N6+ K-K2 19. BxQ KxB 20. Q-B7+ and White should win.

| 15. NxKP!! | BPxN |

If 15. ... RPxN, then 16. BxP+ K-K2 17. N-B7 QxN 18. QxP+ and mates.

| 16. B-N6+ | K-K2 |
| 17. Q-QR3 | |

Checkmate eliminates all resistance.

65. *Sicilian Defense*

In classical times a premature P-KR3 was studiously avoided for it was well known that the weakening could very well leave a player open to a devastating sacrifice. One careless move added to the weakening settles the issue.

1. P-K4	P-QB4
2. N-KB3	P-Q3
3. P-Q4	PxP
4. NxP	N-KB3
5. N-QB3	P-QR3
6. B-N5	P-K3
7. Q-Q3	...

An old move favored by Keres. The idea involves attack along the queen file and a quick transfer of the queen for the king assault.

| 7. ... | P-R3?! |

This weakening is not necessary. A simple strategy would be to develop the queen side with 7. ... QN-Q2 followed by P-QN4 and B-N2.

| 8. B-R4 | B-K2 |

Again the above plan could be implemented.

9.	P-B4	QN-Q2
10.	0-0-0	Q-B2
11.	B-K2	P-QN4

After 11. ... N-B4 12. Q-B3 B-Q2 13. P-B5, White stands better.

12.	B-B3	B-N2?

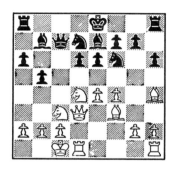

The careless move. Necessary was 12. ... N-B4 13. Q-K2 B-N2 14. P-K5 PxP 15. PxP N-R2 with approximate equality.

13.	NxKP!!	PxN
14.	P-K5!	PxP
15.	Q-N6+	K-B1
16.	BxN	KBxB

After 16. ... NxB 17. BxB QxB 18. PxP, Black still has not solved his problems.

17.	B-R5!	N-B4
18.	PxP	KBxP
19.	KR-B1+	B-B3
20.	P-QN4!!	B-K5

A last desperate stab.

21.	RxB+!	PxR
22.	QxBP+	K-N1
23.	NxB	NxN
24.	QxKP+	

White wins in all variations.

(A) 24. ... K-B1 25. R-B1+ K-N2 26. Q-N6 mate.

(B) 24. ... K-N2 (or ... K-R2 25. Q-N6 mate.) 25. Q-N6+ K-B1 26. R-B1+ K-K2 27. R-B7+ and White wins.

66. *Sicilian Defense*

The bishop is better than the knight. This guidepost necessarily admits of exceptions. Desiring to demonstrate an exception, White, with 14. P-B4, invites the exchange of his bishop for a knight. The point: to keep the position unbalanced. White is too ambitious, and knowing this, Black, fingers and toes crossed, sets the trap!

1.	P-K4	P-QB4
2.	N-KB3	P-Q3
3.	P-Q4	PxP
4.	NxP	N-KB3
5.	N-QB3	P-QR3
6.	B-N5	QN-Q2
7.	B-QB4	Q-R4
8.	Q-Q2	P-K3
9.	0-0	B-K2
10.	P-QR3	P-R3!

The key to coming events. White must choose a permanent post for the bishop. If 11. B-R4, then ... P-KN4 12. B-N3 N-R4 and Black grabs the bishop anyway.

11.	B-K3	N-K4
12.	B-R2	Q-B2
13.	Q-K2	P-QN4
14.	P-B4	N(4)-N5

White sets a trap: 14. ... N-B5 15. N(4)xNP PxN 16. NxP Q-B3 17. QxN!!

15.	P-R3	NxB
16.	QxN	0-0
17.	QR-K1	P-K4!

| 18. N-B5 | BxN |
| 19. PxB | P-Q4! |

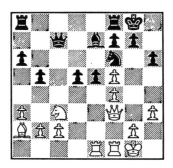

White should now think of saving himself: 20. K-R1 P-Q5 21. QxKP QxQ 22. PxQ PxN 23. PxN BxBP 24. P-QN4! and although Black is better, bishops of opposite colors in this setting should lead to a draw. But White believes he has the edge; so . . .

| 20. QxP?! | B-Q3 |
| 21. Q-K2 | BxRP!! |

First surprise! White's queen side structure is shaken.

| 22. N-Q1 | QR-K1 |
| 23. Q-B3? | . . . |

For better or for worse, 23. Q-Q2 was necessary. Now the trap springs shut.

23. . . .	B-B4+
24. K-R1	RxR!
25. RxR	Q-R4!

Two pieces are attacked; so the reply is forced.

| 26. N-B3 | P-N5! |

Not 26. . . . P-Q5 27. R-R1 PxN 28. BxP+ KxB 29. RxQ PxP 30. Q-N3+, and White escapes.

27. NxP	QxB
28. NxN+	PxN
29. Q-B6	Q-B5

And a piece is enough to win!

67. *Sicilian Defense*

The sacrifice of a piece on Q5 has assumed the label *stock*. White now wishes he had run out of that particular product.

1. P-K4	P-QB4
2. N-KB3	P-Q3
3. P-Q4	PxP
4. NxP	N-KB3
5. N-QB3	P-QR3
6. B-N5	QN-Q2
7. B-QB4	Q-R4
8. Q-Q2	P-K3
9. 0-0-0	P-QN4

The position is double-edged. A likely line is 10. B-N3 B-N2 (... P-N5 11. N-Q5! PxN 12. PxP!) 11. KR-K1 B-K2 12. K-N1 Q-B2 (... 0-0 13. N-Q5!) 13. P-QR3 0-0-0 14. P-B4! with a slight edge for White.

    10. B-Q5?   ...

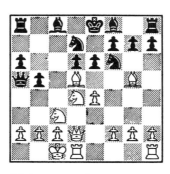

The bishop couldn't resist the magnetic attraction of Q5.

10. . . .	PxB
11. PxP	N-B4!
12. KR-K1+	K-Q2!
13. N-B6	Q-N3
14. P-QN4	N-R5
15. Q-Q3	NxN
16. QxN	N-N5
17. B-Q8	QxP
18. R-B1	Q-K3+!

Convincingly refuting the sacrifice; if 19. QxQ, then NxQ 20. RxP+ K-K1! winning the exchange.

68. *Sicilian Defense*

A *discovery* nets Black a piece—for one move, after which he discovers he comes out a piece down.

1. P-K4	P-QB4
2. N-KB3	P-Q3
3. P-Q4	PxP
4. NxP	N-KB3
5. N-QB3	P-QR3
6. P-B4	. . .

Formerly the most feared continuation because of the rapid king side buildup which it engendered.

6. . . .	P-K4
7. N-B3	QN-Q2
8. P-QR4	P-QN3

While none of Black's last three moves actually loses, there is room for improvement; 6. ... Q-B2 prevents B-QB4 and reserves the possibility of P-KN3 without the sometimes weakening P-K4. Thus, ... Q-B2 is to be recommended on either move seven or eight to put a clamp on White's aggressive king bishop.

| 9. B-B4! | B-K2 |
| 10. 0-0 | 0-0 |

11. Q-K2	B-N2	.
12. PxP	PxP	
13. B-KN5	NxKP?	

The combination works if Black's rook is on QB1 where it eyes the enemy bishop. So why not now play 13. .... R-QB1?

14. NxN	BxN
15. QxB	BxB
16. NxB	QxN

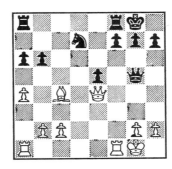

Now White takes advantage of the *overloaded* piece. Black's king rook cannot simultaneously defend his brother rook and the king bishop pawn.

17. RxP!	...

Losing the pawn is not so bad, but the *discovery* situation is fatal. The threat is 18. R-B5+, winning the queen.

17. ...	K-R1
18. RxN	

The extra piece ices the win.

69. *Sicilian Defense*

A common combino refutes a premature P-QN4.

1. P-K4	P-QB4
2. N-QB3	P-Q3

3. N-B3	P-K3
4. P-Q4	PxP
5. NxP	N-KB3
6. P-B4	. . .

Every few years an old move such as the text reappears, not necessarily because it is any better than current fashion, but simply because players tire of the same old hat and find refreshing variety in the past which, hopefully, an opponent will not remember.

6. . . .	B-K2
7. B-K3	P-QR3
8. Q-B3	Q-B2
9. 0-0-0	P-QN4

Capablanca once said, "I see only one move ahead, the best move!" Here Black sees more than one move ahead: 10. P-K5 B-N2 11. PxN BxQ! Unfortunately, there is usually more than one choice in a position.

| 10. P-K5! | B-N2 |
| 11. BxP+! | PxB |

Or 11. . . . K-B1 12. Q-N3 PxB 13. N(4)xNP Q-R4 14. PxN and White wins.

12. N(4)xNP	Q-B1
13. Q-N3	PxP
14. PxP	N-R4
15. Q-R3	P-N3
16. B-R6	. . .

Black indeed has an extra piece, but he cannot castle and his forces are totally disorganized. Meanwhile, White has two pawns for the piece, all his pieces have an aggressive stance, and he already operates with serious threats, e.g., P-KN4 winning a piece.

| 16. . . . | QN-B3 |
| 17. KR-K1 | N-N5 |

Better to seek counterplay with 17. . . . B-R3.

18. P-R3	N-Q4
19. N-Q6+	BxN
20. PxB	RxP?

20. . . . N(R)-B3 spells trouble, but the text courts disaster.

21. P-Q7+!　　　　　. . .

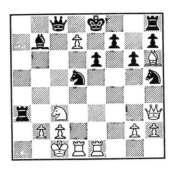

White has conjured up his own fiendish pin!

21. . . .　　　　　QxP

If 21. . . . KxP, 22. PxR anyway.

22. PxR	P-B4
23. NxN	BxN
24. Q-QB3	R-N1
25. P-N4	PxP
26. Q-K5	

Black should surrender; 26. . . . K-B2 27. RxB QxR (27. . . . PxR 28. R-B1+, etc.) 28. Q-B7+ and Black must lose his rook.

70. *Sicilian Defense*

White seizes the initiative and builds a powerful attack against the opposing monarch. Black may hold by solid defense; too bad he is not acquainted with the *clearance theme*. Ignoring the threat against his queen knight, White offers his king pawn too (Move 15!), and it is Black who discovers he must lose a piece.

1. P-K4	P-QB4
2. N-KB3	P-Q3
3. P-Q4	PxP
4. NxP	N-KB3
5. N-QB3	P-QR3
6. P-B4	Q-B2
7. B-Q3	N-B3
8. N-B3	...

Better to avoid exchanges when one has the initiative.

8. ...	P-KN3
9. 0-0	B-N2
10. Q-K1!	...

If Black's king knight can be driven away with P-K5, then White can get in the powerful N-Q5.

10. ...	P-K3
11. K-R1	0-0
12. Q-R4	P-QN4
13. P-B5!	Q-K2
14. B-N5	P-N5??

To prevent P-K5, N-K4 was a must.

15. P-K5!!   **Resigns.**

After 15. ... NxP 16. NxN QPxN (16. ... NPxN 17. N-N4!) 17. N-K4! and Black collapses under the *pin*.

118

71. *Sicilian Defense*

For years the poor *patzer* has stumbled into an inferior line thinking he might have attacking chances: 6. B-K3? N-N5! 7. B-QB4 NxB 8. PxN P-K3 and White's attack is purely speculative. The improvement here forces Black to go back to the drawing boards.

1. P-K4	P-QB4
2. N-KB3	P-Q3
3. P-Q4	PxP
4. NxP	N-KB3
5. N-QB3	P-QR3
6. B-K3!	N-N5?!

An interesting diversion is 6. ... P-K4 7. N-B5?! P-Q4 8. B-N5 P-Q5! 9. N-K2 Q-R4+ 10. B-Q2 Q-N3 and Black is ahead.

7. B-N5!	...

Pinning the king pawn, avoiding Black's king knight and generally hampering Black's development.

7. ...	N-QB3
8. Q-Q2	Q-N3
9. N-N3	P-K3
10. P-KR3	N(5)-K4
11. P-B4	N-N3
12. P-B5	KN-K4

Black has a fine square for his knight, but as for the rest of the pieces, it is White who has the aggressive posture.

13. B-K2	B-Q2
14. B-K3	Q-B2

White has regained the tempo lost on move seven.

15. 0-0	N-R4
16. PxP	PxP
17. NxN	QxN
18. QR-Q1	B-K2
19. K-R1	R-QB1
20. P-R3	R-B3
21. B-R5+!	...

To compel the permanent weakening of the defense with P-N3, or else the surrendering of the right to castle.

21. ...	P-N3
22. B-K2	N-B2
23. B-N4	P-R4
24. B-B3	N-K4
25. B-K2	...

The meddlesome bishop has pried open the treasury guarded by the king side pawns.

25. ...	P-KN4

A trap that boomerangs.

26. BxNP	N-B5
27. Q-Q4	P-K4
28. Q-B2!!	BxB
29. Q-B7+	K-Q1
30. BxN	B-K2
31. Q-N7	R-K1
32. B-B7	R-KB1
33. N-Q5!!	

There is simply no move.

72. *Sicilian Defense*

Obviously, Black spots the catch; yet, thinking there is also a flaw, he falls hook, line and sinker. Satisfactory was 9. . . . Q-B2, after which 10. P-K5 would be met by 10. . . . B-N2.

1. P-K4	P-QB4
2. N-KB3	P-Q3
3. P-Q4	PxP
4. NxP	N-KB3
5. N-QB3	P-QR3
6. B-QB4	P-K3
7. B-N3	P-QN4

Rather than weaken the queen side, Black ought to play 7. . . . QN-Q2, aiming for the QB4 post from which the knight could opt to capture White's pesky bishop at a convenient time.

8. 0-0	B-K2
9. Q-B3	B-Q2?
10. P-K5!	PxP
11. NxKP!!	. . .

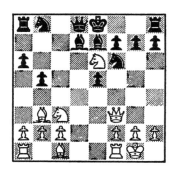

Black expected 11. QxR? PxN 12. N-K4 B-B3 13. NxN+ BxN when he would have fine chances.

11. ...   **P-K5**

After 11. ... PxN, White may safely capture the rook.

12. NxP+   **...**

Not 12. NxKP? PxN 13. NxN+ BxN 14. QxR B-B3 15. Q-R7 B-Q5!, trapping the queen.

12. ...   **K-B1**

Hoping for 13. Q-N3, after which 13. ... P-KR4 stops B-KR6. What does White have in mind?

13. NxKP!!	**B-B3**
14. B-R6!	**BxN**
15. N-R5+	**Black resigns.**

If 15. ... K-K1, 16. NxN+ BxN 17. QxB+ and Black loses his rook; or 15. ... K-N1 16. NxN+ BxN 17. QxQB and the rook goes anyway, since White has the additional threat of Q-N4+.

73. *Sicilian Defense*

A player may be enticed by the immediate gain of material, seemingly with little or no loss to himself. The amateur faces the expert. "I'll lose anyway," laments the amateur, "so I may as well grab the goods and hang on." That's guesswork, not Chess. Beware temptation!

1. P-K4	P-QB4
2. N-KB3	P-Q3
3. P-Q4	PxP
4. NxP	N-KB3
5. N-QB3	P-K3
6. B-QB4	P-QR3
7. B-N3	P-QN4
8. 0-0	B-N2
9. R-K1	QN-Q2
10. B-N5	P-R3
11. B-KR4	N-B4

Black avoids the danger: 11. . . . B-K2 12. BxP! PxB 13. NxKP Q-N3 14. NxP+ K-B2 15. N-B5!

12. B-Q5!! · · ·

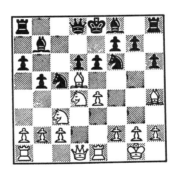

A move of such hypnotic affect that Black feels compelled to capture erroneously. He must now play 12. . . . P-N4. intending 13. . . . Q-N3.

12. . . .	PxB?
13. PxP+	K-Q2

If 13. . . . B-K2, 14. N-B5 wins.

14. P-QN4!! · · ·

The unforeseen crusher. After the impending P-QB4, the Black king will be hopelessly exposed.

14. ...	N-R5
15. NxN	PxN
16. P-QB4!	K-B1
17. QxP	Q-Q2
18. Q-N3	P-N4
19. B-N3	N-R4
20. P-B5!	PxP
21. PxP	QxP
22. R-K8+	K-Q2
23. Q-R4+	B-B3
24. NxB	Black resigns.

74. Sicilian Defense

Weakening the white squares via the attack on the king pawn is the theme.

1. P-K4	P-QB4
2. N-KB3	N-QB3
3. P-Q4	PxP
4. NxP	N-KB3
5. N-QB3	P-Q3
6. B-QB4	P-K3
7. B-N3	B-K2
8. B-K3	0-0
9. 0-0	P-QR3?

Better is 9. ... B-Q2, saving a necessary tempo.

| 10. P-B4! | B-Q2 |
| 11. P-B5! | ... |

Now 11. ... NxN 12. BxN P-K4 13. B-B2 leaves Black paralyzed on the light squares.

| 11. ... | Q-B1? |

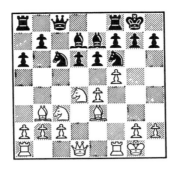

Deluded that this move defends the king pawn. The immediate 11. ... P-K4 does offer fighting chances: 12. NxN PxN!; or 12. KN-K2 (or N-B3) N-KN5!

12. PxP	BxP
13. NxB	PxN
14. N-QR4!	R-QN1

Or else the fork wins the exchange.

| 15. N-N6 | ... |

The queen is nudged away from the defense of the king pawn.

| 15. ... | Q-K1 |
| 16. BxP+ | |

And the rest is a matter of technique.

75. Sicilian Defense

Changing times, changing views.

1. P-K4	P-QB4
2. N-KB3	N-QB3
3. P-Q4	PxP
4. NxP	N-KB3
5. N-QB3	P-Q3
6. B-KN5	B-Q2

7.	Q-Q2	NxN
8.	QxN	Q-R4
9.	P-B4	P-K3
10.	0-0-0	R-B1
11.	P-K5!	...

All this has been seen in the game Hort versus Panno, at Palma de Majorca in 1970. The pawn thrust is a radical attempt to secure an immediate and lasting initiative.

11.	...	PxP
12.	PxP	B-B3!

The king pawn is pinned: 13. PxN QxB+!

13.	B-N5!	...

Breaking the pin: 13. ... BxB 14. PxN and wins.

13.	...	N-Q4
14.	NxN	BxB

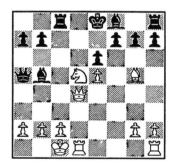

14. ... PxN 15. QxQP, and White wins.

15.	QxP!	...

If 15. ... QxQ, 16. N-B7+ RxN 17. R-Q8 mate.

15.	...	B-N5!

After 15. ... B-R3 16. Q-N6 QxQ 17. NxQ, the extra pawn is the only factor. After the text, White may play 16. QxP!,

but after 16. . . . 0-0 17. NxB QxN, his king would be in great danger.

In the resulting position from Black's 15th turn, if one prefers the two bishops, then he may consider his opponent trapped. But if one prefers the extra pawn, then he may consider that he has caught his man in the opening. The tranquil continuation 16. QxQ BxQ 17. N-K3 seems good, but after 17. . . . R-B4(!) 18. B-B4 (18. P-QN4 RxP!, and not 18. . . . BxP 19. R-Q8 mate.) . . . B-B2 19. P-QN4! R-B3 (19. . . . R-B6 20. K-N2 BxP 21. BxB RxN 22. BxP R-N1 23. B-B6, and White should win.) 20. KR-K1 0-0, and Black has excellent play for the pawn.

Finally, White may try 16. QxQ BxQ 17. P-QN4 PxN 18. PxB, but the resulting pawn weaknesses and the bishops of opposite colors in the ending provide Black sufficient compensation for the pawn.

76. *Sicilian Defense*

Aggressive yet delicate play is required of a player saddled with a weak and isolated queen pawn. Unable to rise to the occasion, Black collapses under the weight of the totally unexpected 14. N-Q5!

1. P-K4	P-QB4
2. N-KB3	P-Q3
3. P-Q4	PxP
4. NxP	N-KB3
5. N-QB3	N-B3
6. B-QB4	P-K3
7. B-N3	B-K2
8. B-K3	0-0
9. Q-K2	. . .

The older continuation is 9. P-B4 followed by 10. Q-B3 when White may still choose to castle king side.

9. ...	Q-R4
10. 0-0-0	NxN
11. BxN	B-Q2
12. K-N1	QR-Q1

More to the point is P-QN4!

| 13. Q-K3! | P-QN3? |

Black avoids the trap with 13. ... P-QN4 14. BxRP R-R1 15. B-N6 Q-R3 with good attacking chances for Black.

| 14. BxN! | PxB |

Naturally BxB loses the queen pawn, but, strangely, that's the lesser evil!

| 15. N-Q5! | ... |

That's all folks! After 15. ... PxN 16. RxP Q-any 17. R-KR5 followed by Q-R6, mate cannot be stopped.

15. ...	KR-K1
16. NxB+	RxN
17. RxP	R-QB1

Escaping the pin, but that's not enough.

| 18. Q-Q4 | B-K1 |
| 19. QxBP | |

Black doesn't like his game—at all!

77. *Sicilian Defense*

Planting a knight on QB5 is the ideal of the defender. Rarely is the ideal accomplished, owing to the intricacy of the opening. We see the "goal" achieved because Black fails to understand why it is so rare and because White wishes to demonstrate the refutation.

1. P-K4	P-QB4
2. N-KB3	N-QB3
3. P-Q4	PxP
4. NxP	N-KB3
5. N-QB3	P-Q3
6. B-QB4	P-K3
7. 0-0	B-K2
8. B-N3	0-0
9. B-K3	P-QR3?!

So far, all this is decent fare. A standard plan is: 9. ... B-Q2 10. Q-B3 NxN 11. BxN B-B3; or 10. Q-Q3 (or Q-B3 as above.) NxN 11. BxN P-QN4 12. NxP BxN 13. QxB NxP when White has the two bishops but Black has the sturdier pawns sweeping down the center.

10. P-B4	Q-B2
11. P-KR3?!	. . .

To prevent N-KN5. Sharper is P-B5!

11. ...	P-QN4
12. P-R3	N-QR4
13. Q-Q3	. . .

Bolstering the all-important king pawn.

| 13. ... | N-B5?? |

Has the knight really arrived? No! Black should have further prepared the maneuver with B-N2 and R-QB1, or else have been satisfied with NxB.

| 14. N(4)xNP! | PxN |
| 15. NxP | ... |

The exposed position of the Black queen triggers the refutation. A pawn in the pocket insures the win.

15. ...	Q-B3
16. QxN	QxQ
17. BxQ	NxP
18. B-Q3	B-N2
19. P-QR4	...

Passed pawns, especially extra ones, must be pushed.

| 19. ... | N-B4 |

The march of the pawns cannot be hampered.

20. BxN	PxB
21. P-R5	KR-Q1
22. KR-Q1	R-Q2?

This hastens the end.

| 23. BxP+! |

White also wins the exchange.

78. *Sicilian Defense*

Against a great player, some experts prefer to exchange queens on the principle that the better player employs his pieces more effectively. Black does not subscribe to this rule of thumb. With 10. . . . P-Q4, he is convinced that he has caught his famous adversary napping, but Fischer is not snared so easily!

1.	P-K4	P-QB4
2.	N-KB3	P-Q3
3.	P-Q4	PxP
4.	NxP	N-KB3
5.	N-QB3	N-B3
6.	B-QB4	P-K3
7.	B-N3	P-QR3
8.	P-B4	Q-R4
9.	0-0	NxN
10.	QxN	P-Q4?!

We prefer B-K2 and castles or Q-QB4 exchanging queens.

11.	B-K3!	NxP
12.	NxN	PxN
13.	P-B5!!	Q-N5

Now, too late, milady would like a casual exchange, for after 13. . . . PxP 14. B-R4+ P-N4, 15. Q-Q5 wins.

14.	PxP!	...

A *zwischenzug* (German Chess parlance meaning in-between or preparatory move.), for if 14. . . . QxQ, then first the the reply 15. PxP+ followed by the recapture of the queen.

14.	...	BxP
15.	BxB	PxB

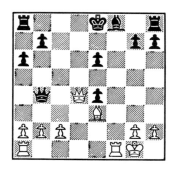

Now a simple exchange sacrifice strips Black of any defense.

16. RxB+!!	QxR
17. Q-R4+!	P-N4
18. QxKP	

And after 18. ... R-Q1 19. Q-B6+ R-Q2 20. B-B5 Q-B2 21. R-Q1, Black is helpless.

79. *Sicilian Defense*

Frequently Black rules the queen bishop file. Here White is waiting.

1. P-K4	P-QB4
2. N-KB3	P-K3
3. P-Q4	PxP
4. NxP	N-QB3
5. N-QB3	P-Q3
6. B-K2	N-B3
7. 0-0	B-K2
8. B-K3	0-0

Willingly or unwillingly, Black has transposed into the Scheveningen Variation.

9. P-B4	B-Q2
10. N-N3	P-QR4
11. P-QR4	P-K4
12. K-R1	N-QN5

Correct is . . . N-QR4, blocking White's queen rook pawn and intending N-QB5.

13. B-B3	R-B1?!

The rook should lay behind to defend the queen rook pawn.

14. R-B2	R-B5?

Leaving room for the queen but fatally misplacing the rook.

15. PxP!	PxP
16. R-Q2	Q-B2
17. Q-KN1	B-Q1

The threat was B-N6 winning the queen rook pawn.

18. QR-Q1	B-B3

The rook is completely entombed.

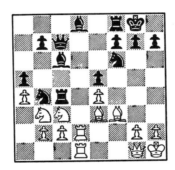

19. B-B5!	R-K1
20. Q-B1!!	

The exchange and the game is lost.

80. *Sicilian Defense*

Moving a knight in the opening not once, twice, thrice, but four times deserves decisive and speedy punishment. In this example there is retribution indeed, but in an exquisite manner.

1. P-K4	P-QB4
2. N-KB3	P-K3
3. P-Q4	PxP
4. NxP	N-KB3
5. N-QB3	P-Q3
6. B-K2	B-K2
7. 0-0	0-0
8. B-K3	N-B3

Once!

| 9. P-B4 | Q-B2 |

The Black set-up is geared to delay P-K5.

| 10. K-R1 | P-QR3 |

The latest *book* on this line offers 11. Q-K1 B-Q2 12. Q-N3 NxN (or ... P-QN4 13. P-QR3.) 13. BxN B-B3 14. B-Q3 P-KN3 15. P-K5 PxP 16. BxKP Q-R4 with approximate equality.

| 11. P-QR4?! | ... |

Preventing P-QN4 but leaving a weakness on his own QN4.

| 11. ... | N-QR4? |

Twice! "Knight on the rim equals trim!" (Tinsley, circa 1880.) Black allows free reign to White's centralized knight; instead he should play 11. ... R-Q1, preparing for his own break which may be either P-Q4 or P-K4, depending on the situation.

| 12. Q-Q3! | ... |

Simultaneously preparing the assault and preventing N-B5.

| 12. ... | B-Q2 |
| 13. P-KN4! | K-R1?! |

Slightly better was ... KR-B1 14. P-N5 N-K1. The text prepares a retreat for the knight but with the knight living in the king-haven, that castle becomes a crowded tenement.

| 14. P-N5 | N-N1 |
| 15. R-B3! | N-QB3? |

Thrice! Perhaps 15. .... P-B3 may give some relief.

| 16. R-KN1!! | NxN? |

Every knight move made White's attack that much more virulent.

| 17. BxN | P-B4 |

An attempt to block the position.

| 18. R-R3 | P-K4? |

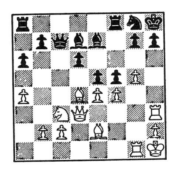

Black is cramped and far behind in development; yet he opens the position!

19. N-Q5!	Q-Q1
20. BPxP!	BPxP??
21. P-K6!!	

An elegant queen sacrifice. One possibility is 21. ... PxQ 22. BxP (Threatening mate.) P-R3 23. PxP NxP 24. RxN+ K-N1 25. RxP mate. If 21. ... BxKP, then 22. Q-QB3 (Threatening mate.) R-B2 23. P-N6! BxR (or ... N-B3 24. N-B4 renewing the mating threats.) 24. QxB (or PxR etc.) N-B3 25. PxR with eventual mate.

81. *Sicilian Defense*

The opening line varies as White has fianchettoed his king bishop but the problem is the same. White is drawn into the trap precisely because he takes for granted the validity of the *sac* of the knight on Q5.

1.	P-K4	P-QB4
2.	N-KB3	P-Q3
3.	P-Q4	PxP
4.	NxP	N-KB3
5.	N-QB3	P-K3
6.	P-KN3	. . .

Aiming to prevent the fianchetto maneuver of Black's queen bishop.

6.	. . .	B-K2
7.	B-N2	0-0
8.	0-0	P-QR3
9.	B-K3	. . .

More active is 9. P-N3 and B-N2, anticipating Black's intention of posting a knight on QB5 and pointing the queen bishop directly toward the enemy king.

9.	. . .	Q-B2
10.	Q-K2	N-B3
11.	QR-Q1	B-Q2

Providing the option of posting the bishop on the long diagonal by . . . NxN and . . . B-B3.

12.	P-KR3	P-QN4
13.	P-R3	KR-B1
14.	P-B4	QR-N1
15.	NxN	BxN
16.	B-B1	. . .

Attack backwards! Especially against World Champion Boris Spassky. To the point is P-KN4-N5.

16. ...	P-QR4
17. KR-K1	P-N5!
18. PxP	PxP

It is surely possible to retreat without fear of instant disaster but White has already spotted a "clever" riposte which apparently regains the initiative.

| 19. N-Q5?? | PxN! |
| 20. PxP | ... |

Two pieces hang. When White picks up one of them, the balance will be his.

| 20. ... | B-Q2! |

But that is not to be, for if 21. QxB, R-K1 wins the queen.

82. *Sicilian Defense*

The queen came out too soon. A player presently ranked among the world's top ten thought he was good enough to make an exception to the rule.

1. P-K4	P-QB4
2. N-KB3	P-K3
3. P-Q4	PxP
4. NxP	P-QR3
5. B-Q3	...

Very flexible, allowing for the possibilities of N-QB3, N-Q2 or P-QB4.

     5. ...   B-B4

A new attempt to create counterplay. The bishop, though less active on K2, sometimes contributes better to the defense. One must use his judgment.

6.	N-N3	B-R2
7.	P-QB4	N-QB3
8.	0-0	Q-R5?

Correct is P-Q3 and Q-B2. The text puts the queen out on a limb.

     9. N(1)-Q2!   KN-K2?

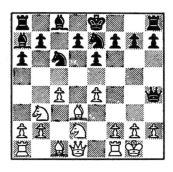

Mandatory was P-Q3.

     10. P-B5!   ...

The bishop is locked in and the queen locked out.

10.	...	N-K4
11.	B-K2	P-QN3
12.	P-B4	N(4)-B3

Here's an interesting line: 12. ... PxP 13. PxN P-B5+ 14. K-R1 PxN 15. P-N3, and now:
   (A) 15. ... Q-R6 16. B-N4 Q-R3 17. N-B4 P-N4 (17. ...

Q-N3 18. N-Q6+ K-B1 19. B-R5 traps the queen.) 18. N-Q6+
K-B1 19. RxP+ K-N1 20. RxN etc.

(B) 15. ... Q-R3 16. N-B4, as in line (A).

13. N-B4	PxP
14. P-N3	Q-R3
15. P-B5	Q-B3
16. PxP	QxKP
17. N-Q6+	K-B1
18. B-QB4!!	

Immense loss of material ensues.

83. *Sicilian Defense*

An over-ambitious king bishop decides to wrest the lime-
light from his colleague by blocking the queen pawn. The
coup involves luring the enemy into perpetrating what he
believes is an opportune pin.

1. P-K4	P-QB4
2. N-KB3	P-K3
3. P-Q4	PxP
4. NxP	P-QR3
5. B-Q3	N-QB3
6. B-K3	N-B3
7. 0-0	Q-B2
8. N-QB3	B-Q3?!

A nice place to visit but a bishop shouldn't live there. The
system is a recommendation of Taimanov who certainly had no
intention of erecting a permanent memorial on Q3.

9. K-R1	P-KR4

After 9. ... BxP, 10. P-KN3 traps the bishop.

10. P-B4	N-KN5
11. Q-B3	NxB?!

139

White should be encouraged to waste a tempo with P-KR3 before effecting this capture.

12. QxN   **Q-N3**

There is the impression that White is caught in his own web.

13. N(3)-K2   **P-K4?**

Expecting 14. PxP BxP 15. P-B3 P-Q3 after which Black has quite a satisfactory position.

14. Q-N3!!   ...

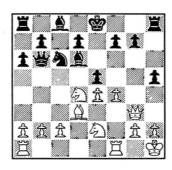

In the style of Alekhine—or even Tal?

14. ...   **PxN**

Black could have refused the piece with 14. ... P-N3 15. NxN PxP 16. NxP QxN! 17. P-K5 B-K2. No one, but no one, could have foreseen the coming events.

15. QxP	**R-B1**
16. P-K5	**B-K2**
17. P-B5	**P-B3**
18. N-B4!	**R-B2**

After 18. ... PxP 19. N-Q5 Q-R4 (19. ... Q-B4 20. N-B7+) 20. NxB NxN 21. P-B6 N-B3 (21. ... R-B2 22. Q-R8+ R-B1 23. P-B7+!) 22. B-N6+ spells Black's end. And after 18. ... NxP 19. QxB+ KxQ 20. N-Q5+ K-Q1 21. NxQ, White is much better.

| 19. PxP! | N-K4 |

Or 19. ... RxQ 20. PxR K-B2 21. P-B6 P-Q3 22. N-Q5 Q-R4 23. PxB+ and a pawn promotes.

| 20. B-B4!! | ... |

No matter how many White pieces hang, the Black goose hangs high.

20. ...	NxB
21. Q-N8+	B-B1
22. NxP!	...

Black can hold after 22. QR-K1+ N-K6(!).

22. ...	N-Q3
23. QR-K1+	K-Q1
24. R-K7!	Q-N4
25. KR-K1	Q-Q4
26. N-B4	QxRP
27. N-K6+	QxN

After 27. ... PxN 28. RxR NxR 29. QxB+ K-B2 30. QxN+ K-N3 31. PxP, White eventually queens a pawn.

| 28. PxQ | RxP |
| 29. R-B7 | |

And Black loses every piece presently developed.

84. *Sicilian Defense*

The continuing saga of White's P-K5 break: if successfully accomplished, White frequently wins in a quick *blitz*; if unsuccessfully, then Black not only wards off all danger, but, more often than not, he builds a big game. Below we witness a sparkling display of such a *big game*.

| 1. P-K4 | P-QB4 |
| 2. N-KB3 | P-K3 |

3. P-Q4	PxP
4. NxP	P-QR3
5. B-Q3	Q-B2
6. 0-0	N-KB3
7. Q-K2	P-Q3
8. P-KB4	QN-Q2
9. K-R1	...

Squandering time; better is 9. B-K3 or P-QR4.

| 9. ... | B-K2 |
| 10. N-QB3 | P-QN4 |

In this setting the pawn break appears most attractive; so ...

11. P-K5?	PxP
12. PxP	QxP
13. Q-B3	B-Q3!

The tempo gained by the mating threat holds together a precarious position.

14. P-KN3	R-QN1
15. N-B6	B-N2
16. B-K4	QxN!!

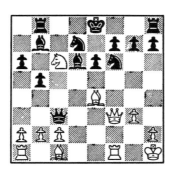

White has fine chances after 16. ... BxN 17. BxB Q-KB4 18. QxQ PxQ 19. R-Q1.

| 17. QxQ | NxB |
| 18. QxP | ... |

White's problems are insurmountable after 18. Q-B3 BxN 19. QxP+ K-Q1(!).

| 18. ... | R-KB1 |
| 19. B-K3 | ... |

Or 19. NxR N-B7+ 20. K-N1 N-R6 mate.

19. ...	BxN
20. K-N1	B-K4
21. QxP	BxP

The three pieces are too much for the queen.

Now we return to the above diagram to give White another try.

17. PxQ	N-K4!
18. NxN	BxB
19. QxB	NxQ
20. NxP	...

Black never considered the fork. Or did he?

| 20. ... | 0-0! |

The pin wins!

| 21. R-K1 | N-B7+ |
| 22. K-N2 | RxN |

Again Black wins handily. You may ask, "What about 18. Q-N2 or 18. Q-B4?"

18. Q-N2: NxB! 19. NxR BxN and there is no solution to 20. ... N-Q3!

18. Q-B4: NxB 19. NxN N-B7+ 20. K-N1 N-R6 mate!

85. *Sicilian Defense*

By snatching a pawn, Black neglects his development, and inherits a dark-square weakness. In concert the double-draw-back is fatal.

1. P-K4	P-QB4
2. N-KB3	P-K3
3. P-Q4	PxP
4. NxP	P-QR3
5. N-QB3	Q-B2
6. B-K2	N-KB3
7. 0-0	B-N5

Black desires to double White's pawns by the tempo–gaining attack on the king pawn. 7. ... B-K2, defending the dark squares around the king is less ambitious but safer.

| 8. B-KN5! | BxN |
| 9. BxN! | ... |

White returns the compliment. Black's pawns will also be weakened and it is he who will be burdened by a serious development deficit.

| 9. ... | PxB |

Not 9. ... BxP 10. BxNP BxR 11. BxR B-B6 12. Q-Q3(!) and White threatens both NxKP and P-K5.

| 10. PxB | QxP?! |

Better is 10. ... Q-KB5 or 10. ... N-B3.

| 11. R-N1 | N-B3 |
| 12. NxN | QPxN? |

Opening the queen file is disastrous. After 12. ... NPxN 13. R-N3 Q-B4 14. K-R1, White has excellent prospects, but still he must prove the worth of the sacrifice.

| 13. R-N3 | Q-B4 |
| 14. Q-Q2 | P-KR4 |

Black does not wish to allow 15. Q-R6.

| 15. R-Q1! | K-K2 |

15. ... K-B1 16. Q-Q8+ K-N2 17. R-N3+, etc.

| 16. R-Q3 | Q-N3 |
| 17. P-K5!! | |

One variation is 17. ... PxP 18. Q-N5+ K-B1 19. R-Q8+ and mate next.

86. *Sicilian Defense*

One side has castled, the other dare not. Develop minor pieces before major ones [B-K2! and not 12. ... R-B1(?)].

1. P-K4	P-QB4
2. N-KB3	N-QB3
3. P-Q4	PxP
4. NxP	P-QR3
5. N-QB3	P-K3
6. B-K2	Q-B2

A current system has transposed into the old Paulsen Variation. Black keeps the line modern by an early P-QN4.

7. P-B4	NxN
8. QxN	N-K2
9. B-K3	P-QN4

The immediate gain of tempo, N-B3, would be premature since White could clog up the queen side with Q-N6.

| 10. O-O-O | . . . |

A matter of temperament: 0-0-0 is usually considered aggressive, while 0-0 is more often evaluated as a positional move.

10. ...	N-B3
11. Q-Q2	B-N2
12. B-B3	...

A fine waiting move, for Black is headed full steam for the *attack*.

12. ...   R-B1??

One should not construct a castle in the middle of the road—particularly the road needed for the queen's retreat.

13. B-N6!!

Black's queen is lost; if 13. ... QxB, 14. QxP mate.

87. *Sicilian Defense*

The tried-but-true constantly returns to the arena. This gem is a trap for all ages.

1. P-K4	P-QB4
2. N-KB3	P-Q3
3. P-Q4	PxP

4. NxP	N-KB3
5. N-QB3	P-KN3
6. B-K2	

An old move returning to prominence.

6. ...	B-N2
7. 0-0	0-0
8. N-N3	N-B3
9. K-R1	B-K3

Intending the freeing P-Q4.

| 10. P-B4 | N-QR4?! |

10. ... Q-B1, preventing 11. P-B5, is the better alternative.

| 11. P-B5! | B-B5? |

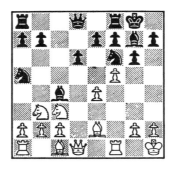

The only recourse was 11. ... B-Q2. But at the moment everything seems so rosy, for if 12. NxN, simply ... BxB first.

| 12. P-K5!! | N-K1 |

White wins a pawn after 12. ... N-Q2 13. PxQP; after 12. ... PxKP 13. QxQ, the knight on QR4 is lost.

| 13. PxP | NxP? |

White's position is immensely superior after 13. ... PxQP 14. N-Q5, but Black would have a fighting chance. Now for the knockout!

| 14. P-B6!! | BxP |

Naturally White wins a piece after 14. ... PxP 15. NxN.

15. NxN	QxN
16. RxB!	BxB
17. NxB	PxR
18. QxN	Q-K8+
19. N-N1	KR-Q1
20. QxP	R-Q8
21. B-K3!!	...

Black may capture the defending bishop only at the cost of his rook; so his reply is forced.

| 21. ... | RxR |
| 22. B-Q4 | QxN+ |

A good try, but this does not save the day. If 22. ... K-B1, 23. Q-R8+ wins a rook.

| 23. BxQ | R-K1 |
| 24. P-KR3 | ... |

The king threatens to escape the pin.

24. ...	R(1)-K8
25. Q-Q8+	K-N2
26. Q-Q4+	K-R3
27. QxP!	

And now White will gladly take two rooks for his queen, since the king and pawns ending a pawn up wins easily.

88. *Sicilian Defense*

The temptation to double an enemy pawn impels the defender to violate another rule: moving a piece twice in the opening. Yet all is not lost—until the king panics.

| 1. P-K4 | P-QB4 |
| 2. N-KB3 | P-Q3 |

3. P-Q4	PxP
4. NxP	N-KB3
5. N-QB3	P-KN3
6. B-K3	B-N2
7. B-QB4?!	...

Permitting a weakening in return for some initiative.

| 7. ... | N-N5?! |

Safer is N-QB3.

| 8. B-N5+ | K-B1 |

Any interposition on Q2 is met by QxN.

9. 0-0	NxB
10. PxN	P-K3
11. B-B4	Q-K2

Defending the king pawn.

| 12. N(3)-N5 | K-N1?? |

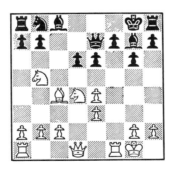

Only B-K4 holds. There would follow 13. N-KB3 N-B3 14. NxB PxN 15. Q-B3 K-N2 16. QR-Q1 and White is slightly better.

| 13. NxQP! | QxN |
| 14. NxP!! | QxN |

There is nothing else: 14. ... QxQ 15. QRxQ N-B3 16. N-B7 R-N1 17. BxP+ K-B1 18. B-N3 discovered check! K-K2 19. R-B7 mate!

15. Q-Q8+	B-B1
16. RxP!	KxR
17. QxB	QxB
18. QxQ+	K-N2
19. Q-Q4+	K-N1
20. Q-Q5+	K-N2
21. QxP+	

And a rook goes too!

89. *Sicilian Defense*

Swallowing the poisoned queen knight pawn is the only antidote. A draw too can be a bonus!

1. P-K4	P-QB4
2. N-KB3	N-QB3
3. P-Q4	PxP
4. NxP	P-KN3
5. N-QB3	B-N2
6. B-K3	N-B3
7. B-QB4	P-Q3
8. P-B3	Q-N3!?

Black is aware that 9. B-QN5 Q-B2 presents no problem.

9. N-B5!?	QxP!
10. NxB+	K-B1
11. K-Q2?!	...

A prepared innovation based on the conclusion that the older 11. N-Q5 offers no advantage.

| 11. ... | KxN! |

The queen must fend for herself. After 11. ... Q-N5 12. B-KR6 QxB 13. N-R5+ K-K1 (best.) 14. NxN+ PxN 15. N-Q5, White clearly stands better.

| 12. P-QR3! | N-QR4 |
| 13. Q-K2 | ... |

With the enormous threat of 14. KR-QN1.

| 13. ... | B-K3!! |
| 14. BxB | ... |

Why not? If 14. ... PxB, 15. KR-QN1 (anyway) N-N6+ 16. K-Q3 ends the battle.

14. ...	KR-QB1!!
15. BxR	RxB
16. R-R2	...

Probably 16. KR-QN1 QxN+ 17. K-Q1 N-B5 18. B-B1 (18. B-Q2, then Q-Q5.) represents a better try, but Black still has at least even odds.

16. ...	QxN+
17. K-Q1	N-B5
18. B-Q2	N-N7+
19. K-K1	Q-K4!

White wins after 19. ... QxBP? 20. RxN QxR? 21. B-R6+!! The awkward position of White's pieces guarantees Black adequate compensation for the exchange and, if he is in a fighting mood, he may fight on for the win.

90. *Sicilian Defense*

Both sides seek the end of the rainbow. Deluded and dismayed, Black sits a queen up, only to find that he has really reached the end of his rope.

1. P-K4	P-QB4
2. N-KB3	P-Q3
3. P-Q4	PxP
4. NxP	N-KB3
5. N-QB3	P-KN3
6. B-K3	B-N2
7. P-B3	N-B3
8. Q-Q2	B-Q2
9. 0-0-0	Q-R4

A queen opposite her opposite sheltered behind a screen always sits on a powderkeg.

10. K-N1 ...

Subsequent capture of the White queen will be accomplished without check—very important, for this will make the un-screening threat all the more dangerous.

10. ... **QR-B1**

Usually the logical continuation is ... 0-0 followed by KR-B1, leaving Q1 open for the queen's retreat, and the rooks permanently connected.

11. P-KN4 **P-KR3?!**

If the intention is ever to castle, the text is a mistake, since it voluntarily provides a target for the bishop and queen which are already conveniently aligned.

12. P-KR4	P-R3
13. B-K2	N-K4
14. P-N5	PxP
15. PxP	RxR?

Admit White has the better game and dig in for the defense with . . . N-R4. The casual exchange loses.

| 16. PxN! | RxR+ |

With check! But is that enough?

| 17. NxR!! | QxQ |

Without check! And here that is much more important.

18. PxB!	K-Q1
19. P-N8=Q+	K-B2
20. QxR+	

Two pieces to the good is quite enough.

91. *Sicilian Defense*

A World's Championship Contender fell into this one. We omit names, dates and places to protect the innocent.

1. P-K4	P-QB4
2. N-KB3	N-QB3
3. P-Q4	PxP
4. NxP	P-KN3
5. N-QB3	B-N2
6. B-K3	N-B3
7. B-QB4	0-0
8. B-N3	. . .

Here we are. Black thinks a moment, all too brief, and then....

8. ...   N-QR4??
9. P-K5!   N-K1

Black spots one trap: 9. ... NxB 10. PxN NxR 11. PxB NxP+ 12. QxN KxP 13. P-KR4 and with two pieces for a rook already in hand White's attack would be irresistible.

10. BxP+!!   ...

"I suspected as much, but too late," laments Black.

10. ...   KxB

If 10. ... RxB, 11. N-K6 wins the queen anyway.

11. N-K6!!   Black resigns.

Naturally, 11. ... PxN loses the queen. After 11. ... KxN mate follows: 12. Q-Q5+ K-B4 13. P-N4+ KxP 14. R-N1+ K-R4 15. Q-Q1+ K-R5 16. Q-N4 mate.

92. *Sicilian Defense*

In the early part of the game, the problem for the second player is to equalize. White has the first move and so, temporarily, the initiative. Problem number two is knowing when one has indeed equalized. Such integrity will not permit a player to panic under pressure. White employs the correct psychology. Simplifying exchanges usually lead to an even game. White *helps* Black avoid complications by tempting his 11. . . . NxN(?). Sadly, Black gives in to temptation!

1. P-K4	P-QB4
2. N-KB3	P-Q3
3. N-B3	N-QB3
4. P-Q4	PxP
5. NxP	P-KN3
6. B-QB4	B-N2
7. B-K3	N-B3
8. P-B3	0-0
9 Q-K2	N-QR4!

Black has equalized! White must either give up his attacking bishop or with it block the queen file.

10. B-Q3	N-B3!

White with the first move ought to lead the way; so Black marks time by recentralizing the knight.

11. 0-0-0	NxN?

Too simple! Both 11. . . . N-K4 and P-Q4 offered excellent play. Now White has what he wanted.

12. BxN	B-K3

Black begins a futile defense of the Q4 square.

13. B-B4!	BxB
14. QxB	P-K3

Necessarily weakening the queen pawn to provide against the threat of 15. P-K5.

15. K-N1	Q-R4
16. Q-N5	Q-B2

Exchanging queens loses the queen pawn.

17. Q-N5	P-KR3
18. Q-R4	P-KN4

19. Q-B2	Q-B5
20. P-KR4!	P-N5
21. Q-N3!	P-N4

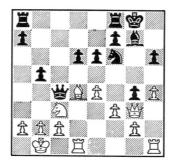

Black sets a trap into which White is only too glad to fall.

22. QxQP	NxP
23. NxN	KR-Q1
24. BxB!!	RxQ
25. NxR	Q-K7
26. B-B3	QxNP
27. KR-N1	QxP
28. QR-KB1	Q-K6
29. RxP+	Black resigns.

93. *Sicilian Defense*

The setting is familiar: the pesky bishop on QB4 and a clear lesson for Black. Next time he'll know that P-K3 is necessary to limit White's king bishop.

1. P-K4	P-QB4
2. N-KB3	N-QB3
3. P-Q4	PxP
4. NxP	N-B3
5. N-QB3	P-Q3
6. B-QB4	P-KN3?

Try the Dragon Variation on another day, or after first preparing with B-Q2.

| 7. NxN | PxN |
| 8. P-K5! | . . . |

Observe! A) 8 ... PxP 9. BxP+ winning the queen.

B) 8 ... N-Q2 9. PxP PxP 10. 0-0 and because of the threat of R-K1+, the plan of posting the bishop on KN2 is thwarted.

C) 8 ... N-N5 9. B-B4 Q-N3 10. Q-B3 B-B4 11. PxP PxP 12. 0-0-0 P-Q4 13. KR-K1+ with various winning ways.

| 8. . . . | N-R4 |
| 9. Q-B3 | P-K3 |

After 9. . . . P-Q4 10. NxP! PxN 11. BxP, it's mate or the rook, or both!

10. PxP	QxP
11. 0-0	B-QN2
12. R-Q1	Q-B4
13. Q-Q3	Q-K2
14. B-KN5!	P-B3

Black was obliged to weaken his king position or be mated immediately.

| 15. B-K3 | K-B2 |
| 16. Q-Q7! | B-B1 |

The threat was B-B5, winning a piece.

| 17. BxP+ | . . . |

Being a pawn down in an ending is like falling off a cliff in slow motion. Black resigns, or else there would be more to come—off!

94. *Sicilian Defense (Closed Variation)*

In this opening the normal square for the White king knight is K2. When White varies, Black fails to smell a rat.

1. P-K4	P-QB4
2. N-QB3	N-QB3
3. P-KN3	P-KN3
4. B-N2	B-N2
5. P-Q3	P-K3
6. B-K3	P-Q3
7. Q-Q2	. . .

White hopes to exchange Black's best defensive piece, the king bishop.

    7. ...   R-N1?!

Delaying the development of the king knight to prevent B-R6, but choosing a routine move which loses valuable time. ... N-Q5 is best.

    8. N-B3!   . . .

Cleverly anticipating the impending N-Q5.

8. . . .	N-Q5?
9. BxN!	PxB
10. N-N5	P-QR3?!

There is a better alternative but on the surface it is not very appetizing: 10. . . . Q-N3!? 11. Q-N4! K-Q2! (Fischer's suggestion). Now White may continue with the dull 12. Q-N3 (12. P-QR3 P-K4! threatening P-QR3.) 12. . . . P-QR3 13. N-R3 Q-B3 with approximate equality. But much more enticing is 12. P-K5!? BxP 13. NxB+ PxN 14. Q-B8! QxN 15. Q-N7 winning the exchange; however, the game would be far from decided. In this last line Black may play 12. . . . PxP! 13. N-N5 N-R3! and, contrary to appearances, Black is out of the woods with a pawn up. Finally 12. P-QR3 P-K4! 13. N-N5 N-R3 14. Q-B4! with great complications.

11. N(5)xQP

With careful play White should convert his pawn plus into a point plus.

95. *Sicilian Defense*

The offbeat or irregular opening sometimes catches the unwary off guard. Remaining alert, Black equalizes by simple and natural development. Not quite satisfied with the results of the opening, White would like to force matters, and it is he who is caught napping.

1.	P-K4	P-QB4
2.	N-QB3	N-QB3
3.	P-B4	...

A return to an old, offbeat and little analyzed system.

| 3. | ... | P-K3 |
| 4. | N-B3 | P-Q4 |

This rapid buildup confronts the ambitious P-KB4.

5.	B-N5	N-K2
6.	Q-K2	PxP!
7.	NxP	P-QR3
8.	BxN+	...

The bishop had no good retreat.

8.	...	NxB
9.	P-Q3	B-K2
10.	B-K3	P-QN3
11.	0-0	0-0
12.	Q-B2	...

To prevent N-Q5.

| 12. | ... | B-N2 |
| 13. | P-QR3 | ... |

Correct is 13. QR-Q1 and P-B3.

13.	...	Q-B2
14.	QR-K1?!	KR-K1
15.	N-K5?	...

Playing for a trap, but instead falling into one. White hopes for 15. ... NxN 16. PxN when the KB file becomes an asset.

| 15. | ... | P-B4!! |
| 16. | NxN | ... |

Black wins a pawn after 16. N-N3 NxN 17. PxN QxP, since the discoveries of the White queen bishop mean nothing.

   16. ...   QxN

After 17. N-N3 B-R5! Black is better, but still, there is no win. But. . . .

   17. N-Q2??   . . .

Heading for K5 via QB4.

   17. ...   B-R5!

Winning the exchange and the game. If 18. QxB, QxP mate.

96. *Sicilian Defense*

We have a clear demonstration of just how dangerous White's attack can be in the Closed, but not passive, Sicilian, if Black fails to meet the opening with active and accurate defense. Since the defense is so difficult, the inexperienced player may prefer to avoid the line altogether.

1. P-K4	P-QB4
2. P-KB4	N-QB3
3. N-QB3	P-KN3
4. N-B3	P-Q3
5. B-B4	. . .

The standard ploy is 5. B-N5, intending to reduce Black's grip on Q4 (Black's Q5) by eliminating the knight. In that case White would also like to cripple the enemy pawns by forcing a recapture on QB6 with the queen knight pawn.

| 5. ... | B-N2 |
| 6. 0-0 | P-K3?! |

Temporarily limiting the scope of the rival bishop, but allowing a dangerous pawn sacrifice.

The preliminary ... N-Q5 is better.

7. P-B5!	KPxP
8. P-Q3	KN-K2
9. Q-K1	0-0?

Asking for trouble; 9. ... N-K4 relieves some of the pressure.

| 10. Q-R4 | Q-Q2? |

Anxious to trade queens, Black misses the chance to simplify with 10. ... B-K3. But this involves returning the pawn, a very unbusinesslike decision.

| 11. B-KR6 | PxP? |

Three or four liberties is more than enough to merit the loss. Returning the pawn with 11. ... P-B5 was the last chance.

| 12. N-KN5 | Q-N5 |

After 12. ... N-B4 13. RxN QxR (13. ... B-Q5+ 14. R-B2!) 14. BxB, and White wins.

13. RxP!!	QxQ
14. RxB+	K-R1
15. RxP	

Black has been checkmated.

97. *Sicilian Defense*

So far we have relied on grandmasters and masters to lead us along the rocky road strewn with pitfalls. Now let's watch a US expert (Col. E. B. Edmondson) throw a US master (United States Chess Federation President, [1969-72] Leroy Dubeck) into a skid.

1. P-K4	P-QB4
2. P-KB4	P-K3
3. N-KB3	P-Q4

The most forthright method of meeting this system marked by 2. P-KB4.

4. B-N5+	B-Q2
5. BxB+	NxB
6. PxP	PxP
7. 0-0	B-K2
8. Q-K2	Q-B2?

Black should prepare to give up castling to escape the pin: 8. . . . KN-B3 9. R-K1 K-B1 10. N-B3 P-KN3.

| 9. N-B3 | KN-B3 |
| 10. R-K1! | 0-0?? |

If White takes the bishop, his queen is trapped—or so Black thinks.

	11. QxB!!	QR-K1
	12. NxP!!	NxN
	13. QxR	RxQ
	14. RxR+	N-B1

Black has paid too much for the queen.

	15. P-Q3	P-KN3
	16. B-Q2	K-N2
	17. QR-K1	N-K3
	18. P-B4	N-B3

This allows a deadly pin but other moves are not much better, e.g., 18. ... N-N3 19. B-B3+ K-R3 20. B-B6 and Black is in a mating net.

	19. B-B3	Q-Q2
	20. R(8)xN!!	PxR
	21. N-N5	QxP
	22. N-K4	

Or 22. NxP+ K-B2 23. N-N5+ K-N2 24. R-K7+ and the Black king is helpless.

98. *Sicilian Defense*

	1. P-K4	P-QB4
	2. P-KB4	P-KN3

3.	N-KB3	B-N2
4.	B-K2	N-QB3
5.	P-B3	P-K3
6.	N-R3	P-QR3
7.	0-0	KN-K2
8.	N-B4	P-Q4
9.	PxP	NxP

Better is PxP followed by 0-0.

| 10. | N(4)-K5 | Q-B2 |
| 11. | NxN | NxKBP?? |

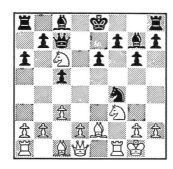

The simple QxN holds the balance.

12.	N(6)-K5!	BxN
13.	NxB	QxN
14.	Q-R4+	...

Instead of winning a pawn Black will get mated.

| 14. | ... | B-Q2 |
| 15. | QxN | QxB |

What else? The piece must be recaptured.

16.	QxP+	K-Q1
17.	P-Q4	Q-N4
18.	Q-B6+	K-B2
19.	Q-K5+!!	

If the king retreats, QxR+; if he advances, QxBP mate.

99. *Sicilian Defense*

The Rossolimo Variation, marked by 3. B-QN5, is a relative of the Ruy Lopez. Here the opposition is lulled into pointless maneuvering until it is too late to save the situation. A totally unexpected sacrifice jolts Black from his inertia.

1.	P-K4	P-QB4
2.	N-KB3	N-QB3
3.	B-N5	P-KN3
4.	0-0	B-N2
5.	P-B3	N-B3
6.	R-K1	0-0
7.	P-Q4	PxP
8.	PxP	P-Q4

This move leads to a balanced position, but also to a static game in which Black must exercise great caution; 8. ... P-Q3 is more fluid.

9.	P-K5	N-K5
10.	N-B3	NxN
11.	PxN	...

White builds his king side action around the strongpoint K5. To counter this action, Black applies pressure on the backward queen bishop pawn.

11.	...	B-Q2
12.	B-Q3	R-B1
13.	N-N5	...

Threatening to disrupt the enemy pawns with P-K6.

13.	...	P-K3
14.	Q-N4	N-K2?

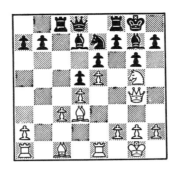

The immediate 15. Q-R4 can be parried by ... P-KR3. White, however, through a timely sacrifice, carries on his attack with gain of tempo. Therefore, correct was 14. ... P-KR3.

15. NxRP!!	KxN
16. Q-R4+	K-N1
17. B-KN5	R-K1
18. R-K3!	RxP

By sacrificing itself for the king bishop, the rook hopes to divert the White rook from the king side, but it is too late.

19. R-R3	RxB
20. Q-R7+!	K-B1
21. B-B6!	N-B4

Neither can mate be avoided after 21. ... BxB 22. PxB N-N1 23. Q-N7 mate; or 22. ... N-B4 23. Q-R8 mate.

22. Q-R8+

And Black is mated on the next turn.

100. *Sicilian Defense*

The idea expressed here has been considered Black's mainstay in this variation. Black drifts into trouble from which he intends to extricate himself by taking advantage of White's king and queen on the same file. The Philidor Theme smashes that hope.

1.	P-K4	P-QB4
2.	N-KB3	N-KB3
3.	P-K5	N-Q4
4.	N-B3	P-K3

There is no objection to 4. . . . NxN.

5.	NxN	PxN
6.	P-Q4	N-B3
7.	PxP	BxP
8.	QxP	Q-N3

Black should confirm his pawn sac with 8. . . . P-Q3, and if then 9. PxP, Q-N3(!).

9.	B-B4!	BxP+

What else?

10.	K-K2	0-0
11.	R-B1	B-B4
12.	N-N5	N-Q5+
13.	K-Q1	N-K3

Black has temporarily succeeded in parrying the threats against his KB2, but now he must face the problem of developing his queen side.

14.	N-K4!	P-Q3
15.	PxP	BxP?

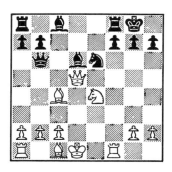

Black should content himself with 15. ... B-Q2, since White will have difficulty introducing his queen rook into play.

| 16. NxB | R-Q1 |
| 17. B-B4! | ... |

The knight is safeguarded by the strangest of quirks, checkmate!

| 17. ... | NxB |

Regaining the piece, but ...

18. QxP+	K-R1
19. Q-N8+!	RxQ
20. N-B7	

Black has been checkmated.

101. *Sicilian Defense*

There should be no quick win. After all, following 12. Q-R4+ B-Q2, Black sees himself unburdened of all fear. Sadly, he is also unburdened of a piece, since White had other plans.

1. P-K4	P-QB4
2. P-QB3	N-KB3
3. P-K5	N-Q4
4. P-Q4	PxP
5. PxP	N-QB3
6. N-QB3	NxN
7. PxN	P-Q3!
8. N-B3	B-N5?!

Preventing 9. P-Q5 with P-K3 followed by B-K2 holds the balance.

| 9. Q-N3?! | R-QN1?! |

Black is far better off after BxN.

| 10. P-K6! | BxP?? |

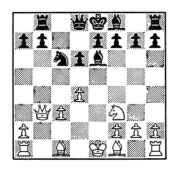

White tossed a pawn to block Black's development. But if Black wants the pawn, he must accept doubled pawns, 10. . . . PxP.

| 11. P-Q5! | N-R4 |

As we said above, "All is well." Except for . . .

| 12. PxB!! | NxQ |
| 13. B-N5+ | |

Lucky thirteen! A couple of pieces behind is enough to get Black down.

102. *Sicilian Defense*

Here we have one of the oldest, yet constantly recurring, traps in the business!

1. P-K4	P-QB4
2. N-KB3	P-Q3
3. P-B3	. . .

To prevent a strong central pawn build-up Black must react quickly with N-KB3. This slows down White's plan since he must stop to defend his king pawn.

| 3. . . . | N-QB3?! |
| 4. P-Q4 | B-N5?! |

The pin doesn't always win.

5. P-Q5!   **N-K4??**

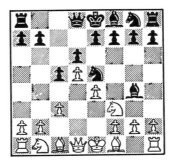

For comparison, let's take a look at the old Nimzovich Defense: 1. P-K4 P-Q3 2. P-Q4 N-QB3 3. N-KB3 B-N5 4. P-Q5! N-K4?? (Correct is N-N1.) 5. NxN! BxQ 6. B-N5+ P-B3 7. PxP Q-R4+ 8. N-B3 and Black cannot handle all the threats.

6. NxN   **PxN**

After 6. . . . BxQ 7. B-N5+ Q-Q2 8. BxQ+ White also has too much.

7. QxB

And Black is minus a piece.

103. *Sicilian Defense*

Right from the beginning the weak point is KB2, for it is there that the king is the lone defender. There are times when a lead in development allows one to ignore threats against that point. Enticed by the weakness, Black embarks upon a sorry pawn-hunt.

1. **P-K4**		**P-QB4**
2. **P-Q4**		**PxP**
3. **N-KB3**		**P-QR3**

| 4. NxP | N-KB3 |
| 5. N-QB3 | P-K4 |

Irregular, but playable. Black must, however, be very careful about the resulting weak light squares.

6. N(4)-K2	B-B4
7. N-N3	P-Q3
8. B-N5	Q-N3?

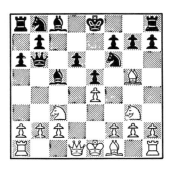

Beginning · a dubious pawn-hunt; B-K3 defends the weak points.

| 9. Q-Q2 | N-N5 |
| 10. 0-0-0!! | NxBP?? |

The end of the pawn-hunt and the game.

| 11. N-Q5 | Q-B3 |
| 12. N-R5! | NxP |

After 12. . . . R-N1, then 13. N-K7.

13. NxP+	K-B1
14. N-R5	NxQ
15. B-K7+	K-K1
16. N(R)-B6	

Black has a queen and a pawn, White has a mate!

104. *Sicilian Defense* (*Morra Gambit*)

The *Pin* that isn't there costs a pawn; the rest is mop-up.

1. P-K4	P-QB4
2. P-Q4	PxP
3. P-QB3	PxP
4. NxP	N-QB3
5. N-B3	P-Q3
6. B-QB4	B-N5??

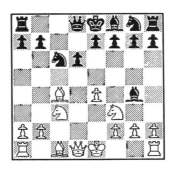

We all love to use that *pin*. But this pin does not win. Just being there was enough for White, and all other winners—sometimes!

7. BxP+	K-Q2

If 7. ... KxB, 8. N-N5+ regains the piece and continues the attack.

8. 0-0	N-B3
9. P-K5!	BxN

Now White demonstrates the use of the true *pin*. If 9. ... NxP, 10. NxN+ and White wins not one but two pieces.

10. QxB	N-K1

After 10. ... NxP, 11. QxP+ wins a rook; and after 10. ... PxP, 11. R-Q1+ is similarly destructive.

11.	B-KB4	R-B1
12.	N-N5	Q-N3
13.	Q-N4+	K-Q1
14.	BxN	QxN
15.	Q-Q7+	

Better to be mated than to remain a total vegetable.

105. *Sicilian Defense*

This was a seven-minute game. Originally, Black had chosen to develop his bishop on K2. Duped by White's apparently passive 3. P-Q3, he changes course and heads for KN2. Needless to say, the loss of time is far more glaring than the defender can afford.

1.	P-K4	P-QB4
2.	N-KB3	P-K3
3.	P-Q3	. . .

Temporarily transposing into the King's-Indian-in-Reverse, But the Opening isn't over yet.

3.	. . .	P-KN3?!

Better to proceed with N-KB3, P-Q4 and B-K2!

4.	P-Q4!	. . .

White can well afford this loss of time—moving the queen pawn twice in the opening—only because of the tremendous weaknesses created by Black's third move. The dark squares will be quite vulnerable.

4.	. . .	B-N2
5.	PxP!	. . .

The defender will lose even more time trying to regain his pawn, thereby giving his rival an enormous lead in development.

5.	. . .	Q-R4+
6.	P-B3!	QxP(4)

Necessary, or else the pawn will be protected by P-QN4.

| 7. **B-K3** | **Q-B2** |
| 8. **N-R3!** | **P-QR3?** |

A gamble, but also inadequate is: 8. ... BxP+ 9. N-Q2! BxP 10. N-N5 Q-R4 11. Q-B2 BxR 12. QxB+ K-K2 13. B-B5+ etc. Naturally not 9. PxB QxP+ and QxN(R3). After 9. ... BxN+, 10. QxB, Black will have his pawn more, but he will meet his end rather swiftly along the dark squares: N-B4-Q6, Q-Q4 and B-KR6.

9. **N-B4!**   ...

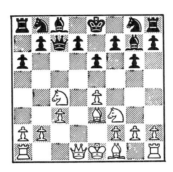

Black cannot prevent N-N6 with great loss of material.

106. *Sicilian Defense*

Helping White castle is part of the scheme. Still, Black must induce another mistake. The *pin* does it again!

| 1. **P-K4** | **P-K3** |
| 2. **P-Q4** | **P-QB4** |

Instead of directly going into a French Defense Black attempts to transpose into the Sicilian.

3. **N-KB3**	**PxP**
4. **NxP**	**N-QB3**
5. **N-QB3**	**P-Q3**

6. B-QB4	N-B3
7. B-KN5	Q-N3
8. BxN	PxB
9. N(4)-N5?	...

Aggressive, but unfortunately the move misplaces the knight. Best is 9. N-N3

9. ...	N-K4
10. B-N3	R-KN1
11. 0-0?!	...

Correct was K-B1, completely avoiding the ensuing pitfall.

| 11. ... | P-QR3!! |

Forcing the knight's retreat to R3 where it will be temporarily out of play.

| 12. N-Q4?? | QxN! |

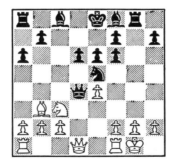

A piece is lost: 13. QxQ N-B6+—the pawn is pinned—14. K-R1 NxQ.

107. *Three Knights Defense*

Seeing this game one can only say *beautiful*! We would be at a great loss had not White gone for the bait at KN4. Now we have a true gem, perhaps often to be repeated in amateur play!

176

1. P-K4	P-K4
2. B-B4	N-KB3
3. N-KB3	N-B3
4. 0-0	. . .

We hate to labor the obvious, but Black was waiting for White to castle!

4. . . .	B-B4
5. P-Q3	P-Q3
6. B-KN5	B-KN5
7. P-KR3	P-KR4!
8. PxB?!	. . .

A question mark because the move loses, an exclamation mark because the refutation is most beautiful.

8. . . .	PxP
9. N-R2	P-N6!
10. N-KB3	N-KN5!
11. BxQ	BxP+
12. RxB	PxR+
13. K-B1	R-R8+
14. K-K2	RxQ
15. KN-Q2	. . .

There is no other way to prevent the promotion of Black's pawn. Notice that White's queen knight is tied down!

15. . . .	N-Q5+
16. KxR	N-K6+
17. K-B1	N-K7

Checkmate is a very convincing conclusion!

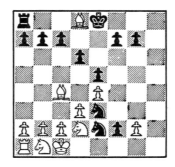

108. *Two Knights Defense*

The obvious often leads to disaster. Having made a natural recapture of material, Black is stunned by the simplicity of 0-0!

1. **P-K4**	**P-K4**
2. **N-KB3**	**N-QB3**
3. **B-B4**	**N-B3**
4. **P-Q4**	**PxP**
5. **N-N5**	**P-Q4**

To black out the enemy bishop.

6. **PxP**	**NxP?**

Inconsistent and disastrous to boot. Black could have neutralized the bishop with N-QR4.

7. **0-0!!**	**B-K2**
8. **NxP!**	**KxN**

The sacrifice must be accepted.

9. **Q-B3+**	**K-K3**

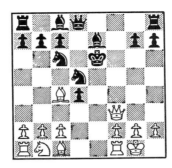

The only hope is to hang on to the ill-gotten gains.

    10. N-B3!   ...

This clearance sacrifice allows the queen rook to enter the fray with gain of tempo.

10. ...	**PxN**
11. R-K1+	**N-K4**
12. B-B4	**B-B3**
13. BxN	**BxB**
14. RxB+	**KxR**

And now for that queen rook!

15. R-K1+	**K-Q5**
16. BxN	**R-K1**
17. Q-Q3+	**K-B4**
18. P-N4+	**KxP**
19. Q-Q4+	

Black cannot avoid checkmate.

109. *Two Knights Defense*

There is frequently the temptation to attack the rival's queen. Here the privilege costs Black the game!

1. P-K4	**P-K4**
2. N-KB3	**N-QB3**
3. B-B4	**N-B3**

4. P-Q4	PxP
5. 0-0	NxP
6. R-K1	P-Q4
7. BxP!	QxB
8. N-B3	

White takes advantage of a *double pin* to regain his piece.

8. . . .	Q-B5?!

The normal Q-QR4 or KR4 are better alternatives.

9. NxN	B-K3

Why not simply B-K2 followed by 0-0?

10. P-QN3	Q-N4
11. NxP	NxN
12. QxN	R-Q1?

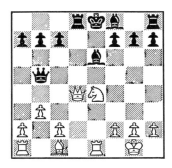

Better to propose the exchange of queens with Q-N3.

13. N-B6+!!	PxN

There is no choice. If 13. . . . K-K2, then 14. B-R3+!

14. QxBP	R-KN1
15. RxB+!!	PxR
16. QxP+	

Resigns, for there will follow 16. . . . B-K2 17. QxR+ K-Q2 18. Q-N4+!! when Black, remaining two pawns behind, still does not get his king into safety.

110. *Two Knights Defense*

Here's a cute companion to the last game. Black desperately desires queen-safety; he'll be braver next time.

1. P-K4	P-K4
2. N-KB3	N-QB3
3. P-Q4	PxP
4. B-QB4	N-B3
5. 0-0	NxP
6. R-K1	P-Q4
7. N-B3	. . .

An exciting alternative to BxP.

7. . . .	PxB

Also playable is 7. . . . PxN 8. BxP B-K3 9. BxN B-QN5.

8. RxN+	B-K3

The alternative 8. . . . B-K2 offers equality: 9. NxP P-B4 10. R-B4 0-0 11. NxN QxQ+ 12. NxQ (Ragosin-Botvinnik, 1930).

9. NxP	NxN
10. RxN	Q-B1?

Correct is 10. . . . Q-B3, and if 11. N-K4, then . . . QxR! 12. QxQ R-Q1!

11. B-N5	B-Q3
12. N-K4	P-KR3

The Black queen is on ice and so is the game. White also wins after 12. . . . 0-0 13. N-B6+ PxN 14. BxP.

13. Q-R5!	Q-Q2

The entrance of the queen is now superfluous.

14. QR-Q1	Q-R5?!

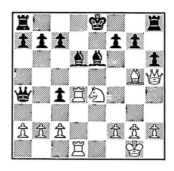

Some practical chances are offered after 14. .... R-KB1.

15. N-B5!   ...

The pretty point; the knight is immune because of mate on the eighth rank. We witness a type of pin with the highest prize behind it, checkmate!

15. ...	P-KN3
16. Q-K2	Q-B3
17. NxB	BxP+
18. K-B1!	...

If 18. KxB, PxB—with check—and then ... PxN, when Black may survive.

18. ...	PxB
19. N-Q8	

Discovered Check! And White tucks the rival queen safely away.

111. *Vienna Opening (Weaver Adams Variation)*

This opening has its ups and downs, but it may never again make the scene, that is, unless Bobby Fischer or some other world master decides to popularize the idea. We recommend the opening for the regular player, not for its great reliability or solidity, but for the countless possibilities of pulling off a quick win.

1. P-K4	P-K4
2. N-QB3	N-KB3
3. B-B4	NxP!

An attempt to throw White off his stride. Else Black may have continued: 3. ... N-B3 4. P-Q3 B-B4 5. B-K3 B-N3 6. KN-K2 P-Q3 7. 0-0 0-0 8. BxB RPxB 9. P-B4 with only a minimal edge for White.

| 4. Q-R5 | . . . |

Black has easy equality after both 4. NxN P-Q4 and 4. BxP+ KxB 5. NxN P-Q4.

| 4. ... | N-Q3 |
| 5. B-N3 | . . . |

The immediate recapture, QxP+, leads to no advantage.

| 5. ... | N-B3 |
| 6. P-Q4?! | . . . |

This and almost every other idea in this opening is long incorporated into old Weaver's analysis. The text involves a temporary pawn sacrifice for quick development.

| 6. ... | PxP |

Better is 6. ... NxP to knock out, if possible, White's king bishop.

| 7. N-Q5 | . . . |

Here we are. With two pawns ahead Black can hardly imagine any danger; so he continues to *secure* his position by *expelling* the enemy queen.

| 7. ... | P-KN3?? |

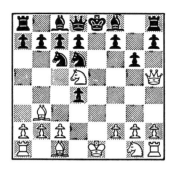

With 7. ... B-K2 White's claims would be severely tested.

8. Q-K2+!	B-K2
9. N-B6+	K-B1
10. B-R6	

Black has been mated.

112. *Benoni Defense*

There's almost a mirror-image and that's the catch, almost! The same move in almost the same position wins in one case and loses in the other. The almost-mirror-image causes the illusion and the downfall.

1. P-Q4	N-KB3
2. P-QB4	P-K3
3. N-QB3	P-B4
4. P-Q5	PxP
5. PxP	P-Q3
6. N-B3	P-KN3
7. P-K4	B-N2
8. B-K2	0-0
9. 0-0	R-K1

Before he advances on the queenside Black must first put pressure on the center.

| 10. N-Q2 | QN-Q2 |
| 11. P-QR4 | ... |

If 11. P-B4, then P-B5! 12. BxP N-B4 13. Q-B2 N-N5! 14. N-B3 Q-N3 15. K-R1 BxN 16. PxB NxKP and Black has a big game.

| 11. ... | N-K4! |
| 12. Q-B2 | ... |

White can protect his pawn immediately with P-B3 but he hopes to be more aggressive and play P-B4 later.

| 12. ... | P-KN4! |

Stabilizing the central post of the knight!

13. N-B3!	NxN+
14. BxN	P-KR3
15. B-Q2	P-R3
16. B-K2	Q-K2
17. P-B3!	...

A realist, White curbs his aggressive intentions of P-B4 and instead protects his pawn.

| 17. ... | Q-K4 |
| 18. K-R1! | Q-Q5? |

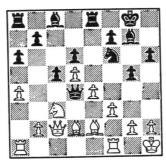

Infected with a wanderlust, the queen gets lost. Correct was the developing move B-Q2.

| 19. N-N5!! | PxN |

If 19. ... Q-K4, then simply 20. N-B7 winning the exchange with a knight fork.

| 20. B-B3!! | Q-K6 |
| 21. BxP! | ... |

Threatening to win a rook with BxN.

21. ...	B-Q2
22. QR-K1	Q-B5
23. P-KN3!	Resigns

The queen has come to a dead end.

113. *Benoni: The Almost-Mirror-Image, Part Two*

Up until now the moves are the same as in No. 112.

17. QR-K1?!

In this example, White refuses to give up his dream of playing the aggressive P-B4.

| 17. ... | Q-K4 |
| 18. K-R1 | Q-Q5!! |

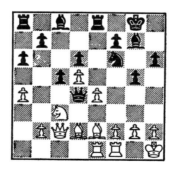

Waiting for his adversary to spring the "trap."

19. P-B3?! ...

Playing for the win, White naturally avoids repeating moves with 19. B-K3 Q-K4 20. B-Q2 Q-Q5 21. B-K3.

| 19. ... | N-R4! |
| 20. N-N5? | |

White springs the trap but he'll find he's falling himself. The difference is that his QR pawn is unprotected now that his rook has moved to K1. The Black queen therefore cannot be trapped.

| 20 ... | PxN! |
| 21. BxQNP | Q-K4!! |

Black gives up the exchange, but he extricates his queen and remains with two pieces for the rook, just enough to win. And enough is enough; White resigns.

114. *Benoni Defense*

An exposed piece on an open file is the theme. The fork makes it work!

1. P-Q4	N-KB3
2. P-QB4	P-B4
3. P-Q5	P-K3
4. N-QB3	PxP
5. PxP	P-Q3
6. P-K4	P-KN3
7. B-KB4	P-QR3!

Avoiding ... B-N2 8. Q-R4+ B-Q2 9. Q-N3 Q-B2 10. N-B3 0-0 11. P-K5 PxP 12. BxP Q-B1 13. B-K2 R-K1 14. 0-0 and Black has trouble unraveling his pieces in view of White's central domination. Or 12. ... R-K1 13. B-K2!

8. P-QR4	B-N2
9. N-B3	0-0
10. B-K2	B-N5!
11. 0-0	R-K1
12. P-R3?	...

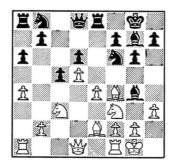

The old-fashioned 12. Q-B2 ably defends the king pawn.

| 12. ... | NxKP! |
| 13. NxN | ... |

After 13. PxB BxN 14. PxB? NxQBP, Black regains the piece with a winning game.

13. ...	RxN
14. B-KN5	Q-K1
15. B-Q3	BxN
16. QxB	R-QN5
17. QR-K1	B-K4
18. Q-Q1	QxP
19. QxQ	RxQ
20. P-B4	B-Q5+

Black has enough material to bring home the bacon.

115. *Benoni Gambit*

A gambit is supposed to give the gambiteer the time he needs to build a crushing attack. Some gambits may be refused; this one definitely must be accepted.

1. P-Q4	N-KB3
2. P-QB4	P-B4
3. P-Q5	P-QN4?!
4. P-QN3?	...

A theoretical novelty, but a poor one. White must take the pawn.

4. ...	PxP!
5. PxP	P-Q3
6. N-QB3	P-N3
7. B-N2	B-KN2
8. P-B3	QN-Q2
9. P-K4	R-QN1
10. Q-B2	Q-R4!

Without cost of the gambit pawn Black has the ideal Benoni, and already White can hardly defend.

| 11. K-B2? | ... |

Ugly, but offering greater opposition is K-Q2. The ensuing combination is a logical consequence of the dark square debility created by the refusal to accept the gambit.

11. ...	NxP+!
12. PxN	RxB!!
13. QxR	BxN
14. Q-B1	N-B3!

Prosperity does not prevent Black from pressing the attack. If 15. B-Q3, BxR 16. QxB Q-Q7+ 17. B-K2 NxP+ is conclusive. Or 15. R-N1 NxP+ 16. K-K2 QxP+ also winning.

| 15. N-B3 | NxP+ |

White would have to be masochistic to continue.

116. *Benoni Gambit*

Offering a pawn for counterplay is common enough. But the finesse which causes panic in the enemy ranks reaps greater dividends.

1. P-Q4	N-KB3
2. P-QB4	P-KN3
3. N-QB3	B-N2
4. P-K4	P-Q3
5. B-N5	P-B4
6. P-Q5	P-N4!

Taking advantage of the temporary absence of the queen bishop from the queen side. If White chooses to decline the sacrifice, then Black will have achieved the break tax-free and will therefore inherit the initiative.

7. PxP	P-QR3
8. N-B3	QN-Q2
9. N-Q2	0-0
10. PxP	Q-N3!

A positional finesse (trap)! Black lures White into attacking the queen. Then when the Black bishop captures the rook pawn, he will already be attacking, and thus in a position to destroy a powerfully posted knight. Consequently, White will remain with a bishop biting on its own pawns 11. Q-B2 avoids this scheme.

11. N-B4?!	Q-N1
12. B-K2	BxP
13. Q-Q2?	. . .

The bluff worked. Correct was 13. P-QN3 BxN 14. BxB Q-N5 15. B-Q2!

13. . . .	BxN!
14. BxB	Q-N5

The queen zooms to the attack with authority.

15. B-Q3	N-K4

In the Benoni, when the defender regains the sacrificed pawn, more often than not, he sits with a won game.

16. K-K2??   ...

A pawn is one thing, a king is another. R-QN1 defends staunchly.

16. ...	**NxB!**
17. KxN	**NxKP!**

18. NxN	**Q-Q5+**
19. K-K2	**QxN+**
20. K-B1	**KR-N1**
21. R-K1	**Q-B5+**
22. Q-K2	**QxQP**

White's king rook is entombed and his queen side pawns fall. Enough!

117. *Bird's Opening*

Because of its rarity, the Bird cannot be dubbed modern. We present examples here, however, since there is a movement afoot to rejuvenate the debut—notably by Larsen, who prefers 1. P-QN3 and a later P-KB4. Lombardy combines P-KB4 with N-KR3, properly timed, and names the opening the Paris

191

Attack. Santasiere, mixing P-QN4 with P-KB4, calls the opening Santasiere's Folly. In each instance, the basic idea is to achieve control of the vital square K5.

1. P-KB4	N-KB3
2. P-QN3	P-KN3
3. B-N2	B-N2
4. P-K3	P-Q3
5. Q-B1	...

If the bishop is not immediately protected, Black may employ the pin to free his game, e.g., 5. N-KB3 P-K4! 6. PxP N-N5!

5. ...	0-0
6. N-KB3	N-B3
7. P-Q3??	...

Violating the principle of rapid development (N-KB3, B-K2 and 0-0), and irreparably damaging the dark squares, particularly K3. White's queen bishop has committed itself to the queen side which fact alone should impel one to weigh carefully any pawn move that might weaken the dark squares on the opposite wing. White wishes to develop a knight on Q2, but prior to this, he should secure the king's position.

7. ...	P-K4!
8. PxP	N-KN5
9. PxP??	...

Biting off more than he can chew. Mandatory was P-KR3.

9. ...	B-R3!!
10. PxP	Q-K1

Now all Black's forces pounce on the weak point. Pawns are of no further importance to either side.

11. B-K2	NxKP
12. N(1)-Q2	NxP+
13. K-B2	Q-K6+
14. KxN	QxB+
15. K-N3	N-K2

And White's fate may be sealed thus: 16. Q-KN1 N-B4+ 17. K-R3 N-K6+ 18. K-R4 N-N7+ 19. K-N3 B-B5 Mate.

118. *Bird's Opening*

In Bridge one *unblocks* a suit by throwing away higher cards of a suit in one hand in order to cash the lower cards in the partnership hand. In Chess the principle is the same. One throws away a piece or a pawn to make some other piece doubly effective, cashing in on that piece.

1. P-KB4	P-QB4
2. N-KB3	N-QB3
3. P-QN3	N-B3
4. B-N2	P-KN3
5. P-K3	B-N2
6. B-K2	0-0
7. 0-0	P-Q4
8. Q-K1?!	...

The theme of a king side attack via Q-KR4 coupled with N-KN5 is not feasible. White should play Q-B1, protecting his queen bishop, thereby rendering relatively ineffective Black's next move.

8. ...	P-Q5!
9. N-R3	...

If 9. PxP, then 9. ... N-Q4 anyway.

| 9. ... | N-Q4 |
| 10. R-Q1?? | ... |

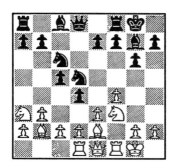

Necessary was P-B4!

| 10. ... | P-Q6!! |

The *unblocking* or clearance sacrifice.

| 11. BxB | PxB! |
| 12. QxP | KxB |

And Black has netted a piece.

119. *Bird's Opening*

1. P-KB4	P-Q4
2. P-K3	N-KB3
3. N-KB3?	...

This permits Black instant equality. Correct is 3. B-K2, followed by P-QN3 and B-N2, which sequence does not facilitate the development of Black's queen bishop.

3. ...	B-N5!
4. B-K2	QN-Q2
5. P-QN3?	...

Totally ignoring the threat; P-Q4, P-B4, or even N-K5 prevents the K4 break.

| 5. ... | BxN! |

The minor exchange, bishop for knight, cannot assume the importance of a central breakthrough.

| 6. BxB | P-K4! |
| 7. PxP?! | ... |

Simply 0-0 is fine.

7. ...	NxP
8. 0-0	B-Q3
9. B-N2	P-B3
10. P-Q3?	...

Although the move is certainly fatal, White finds himself making this error time and again both in the Bird and other analogous positions. N-B3-K2 was in order.

10. ...	Q-B2!
11. P-KR3	P-KR4
12. N-Q2	N(4)-N5!

Again we note the queen bishop vacationing at his queen side resort.

| 13. QBxN | ... |

Or 13. PxN PxP 14. B-K2 B-R7+ 15. K-R1 B-B5+ 16. K-N1 BxP+ etc.

13. ...	B-R7+
14. K-R1	B-N8!
15. P-N3	QxP
16. Q-K2	BxP

And the ensuing QxP+ cannot be handled, for if 17. B-KN2, then Q-R7 checkmate.

120. *Bird's Opening*

The weak light-square complex on the queen side is the passport for White's king side action.

| 1. P-KB4 | P-Q4 |
| 2. P-K3 | P-K3?! |

Compounding the problem of developing the queen bishop. Correct is 2. ... N-KB3.

| 3. N-KB3 | P-QB4 |
| 4. P-QN3! | ... |

White banks his attack on the control of K5.

4. ...	N-KB3
5. B-N2	B-K2
6. B-N5+	B-Q2!
7. B-K2	...

This does not really lose time. When the White knight arrives at K5, he will have a handy target on Q7.

| 7. ... | 0-0 |
| 8. 0-0 | P-QN4?! |

This move makes difficult the normal deployment of N-QB3, since the queen knight pawn will first have to be defended.

| 9. N-K5! | P-QR4 |
| 10. R-B3!! | ... |

With the center secure, White can afford to divert the heavy pieces to the flank for the attack.

10. ...	N-K5
11. R-R3	P-B3
12. NxB	QxN
13. P-QR4!	...

Without his queen bishop Black's queen side action comes to a standstill.

| 13. ... | P-N5? |

Necessary was 13. ... PxP. Now White gains the time needed to bring his queen into play.

14. B-N5!	Q-B1
15. Q-R5	P-R3
16. Q-N6	K-R1

The threat was 17. RxP.

| 17. P-Q3 | N-Q3 |
| 18. N-Q2 | NxB |

There is no time for 18. ... R-R2: 19. R-KB1 followed by R(1)-B3-N3.

| 19. R-KB1! | N-Q3 |

There are two possibilities. I. 19. ... Q-K1 20. RxP+ K-N1 21. Q-R7+ K-B2 22. N-B3(!). II. 19. ... Q-K1 20. RxP+ PxR 21. QxRP+ K-N1 22. R-B3. In either case, White is victor.

20.	RxP+!!	PxR
21.	QxRP+	K-N1
22.	Q-N6+	K-R1
23.	R-B3	P-K4
24.	P-B5!	

To stave off mate, Black must surrender his queen.

121. *Budapest Gambit*

The Budapest is Black's attempt to escape the rigors of positional jockeying necessarily involved in the normal Queen Pawn Opening.

1.	P-Q4	N-KB3
2.	P-QB4	P-K4?!
3.	PxP	N-K5?!

The Budapest is rightly considered unsound but Black does have practical counter-chances after 3. . . . N-N5.

4. P-QR3!   . . .

This move is considered to be the refutation of the Fajaro-wicz Variation (N-K5): 4. . . . N-QB3? 5. N-KB3 P-Q3 6. Q-B2! B-B4 7. N-B3! NxBP 8. QxB NxR 9. P-K6! and White will eventually win the knight in the corner. Black remains a pawn down after 7. . . . NxN 8. QxB N-R5 9. P-K6! (Reshevsky-Bisguier, Rosenwald Tournament, N.Y.C., 1954–55).

4. . . .   P-Q3!

Probably the reason Black plays the line. Instead of Bisguier's 4. . . . N-QB3, which loses time, Black gives up the pawn immediately in order to enhance his development.

5. PxP?!   . . .

Reshevsky's idea still gives White the edge.

5. . . .   BxP

The stage is set. In this opening White often fianchettoes the king bishop to gain greater command of the center. Black waits. . . .

| 6. P-KN3?? | NxBP |
| 7. KxN | . . . |

The fork of the queen and rook compelled this capture.

| 7. . . . | BxP+! |

And Black wins the queen.

122. *Catalan Opening*

A discovered check wins a pawn, but Black should better curtail his predatory instincts!

1. P-QB4	N-KB3
2. N-KB3	P-K3
3. P-KN3	P-Q4
4. B-N2	B-K2
5. 0-0	0-0
6. P-Q4	. . .

Now we have a Catalan; White could have chosen a Reti System with 6. P-N3.

6. . . .	PxP
7. N-K5	P-B4
8. PxP	Q-B2

Black will not swap queens to enter an ending in which he lags in development.

9. NxQBP **BxP?!**

Safer is 9. ... QxBP and the transfer of the queen to the king side.

10. N-B3! **BxP+?**

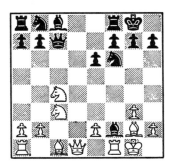

Correct was the sharp R-Q1.

11. RxB **QxN**

Since Black had to recapture his piece, he could not avoid the ensuing exchange sacrifice.

12. RxN!! **PxR**
13. B-R6 **N-B3**

There is no time for R-K1 on account of N-K4.

14. P-K3 **. . .**

Now comes her majesty.

14. . . . **R-Q1**
15. Q-R5 **P-K4**
16. N-K4 **Q-K3**
17. Q-R4

The capture of the king bishop pawn makes mate on R7 inevitable.

123. *Catalan Opening*

An obvious but faulty recapture (13. ... BxP) is bad enough. Then Black smells a pawn which turns out to be a rat.

1.	P-Q4	P-Q4
2.	P-QB4	P-K3
3.	N-KB3	N-KB3
4.	P-KN3	B-K2
5.	B-N2	0-0
6.	0-0	P-B3

More aggressive is ... P-B4.

7.	P-N3	QN-Q2
8.	B-N2	P-QN3
9.	QN-Q2	B-N2
10.	R-B1	R-B1
11.	P-K3	P-B4

Finally the break, but only after squandering a precious tempo (6. ... P-B3).

12.	Q-K2	R-B2

Finding a convenient square for the queen is a problem Black has not solved in this system. The text prepares for Q-R1 and KR-B1.

13.	BPxP	BxP?

Displaying symptoms of drawing fever. Desire for a draw is the worst reason for selecting a passive line. Try ... PxP!

14.	P-K4!	B-N2
15.	P-K5	N-Q4
16.	N-B4	. . .

Avoiding possible exchanges on the open file and eyeing Q6.

16.	. . .	Q-R1?!

Correct is ... PxP 17. BxP (17. NxQP P-QR3) P-QN4! with fighting chances.

17. N-Q6!   **BxN**

There's hardly a choice, for if White captures the queen bishop, the long light diagonal will become a decisive weapon in his hands.

18. PxB	R-B3
19. PxP	PxP
20. N-N5!	RxP
21. KR-Q1	R-R3

Out of one pin.

22. Q-K4!   **. . .**

And into another! The knight on Q4, vital to the king side defense, is paralyzed due to the undefended state of the queen bishop. The weakening of the king side is therefore forced.

22. ...	P-B4
23. Q-QB4!	Q-K1
24. R-K1	RxP

Black finds no relief: 24. ... N(2)-B3 25. QBxN RxB 26. BxN wins a piece.

25. RxKP   **Q-R1**

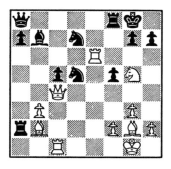

| 26. BxN! | BxB |
| 27. Q-KR4 | P-KR3 |

A fine defense in certain positions.

| 28. QxP!! | N-B3 |

After . . . PxQ 29. R-KN6 is mate.

| 29. RxN |

Black cannot escape material loss and eventual mate.

124. *Catalan Opening*

Superior development does not give license to frivolous sacrifice. The White knight walks in with two left feet and gets unshod in the enemy stable.

1. P-Q4	P-Q4
2. N-KB3	P-K3
3. P-B4	N-KB3
4. P-KN3	B-K2
5. N-B3	0-0
6. B-N2	PxP!
7. 0-0	P-B4
8. Q-R4?	. . .

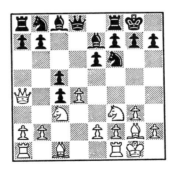

Slightly in White's favor is 8. PxP! QxQ 9. RxQ BxP 10. N-K5! He simply expects too much from the position.

| 8. . . . | PxP! |
| 9. N-QN5 | . . . |

After 9. R-Q1, B-Q2 anyway.

9. . . .	N-B3
10. B-B4	P-QR3!
11. KR-Q1	B-Q2!!

A classic example of the *discovery*. White has no escape.

| 12. N-Q6 | . . . |

Naturally 12. QNxP loses a piece.

| 12. . . . | P-K4! |

The bishop on Q2 encourages such liberties in full view of her majesty.

| 13. NxNP | Q-N3 |
| 14. B-N5 | QxN |

The knight has been corralled. A futile stab would be 15. NxP NxN 16. BxQ BxQ 17. BxR BxR!

125. *Catalan Opening*

Prepared analysis, or just one long series of pitfalls? A lot of both!

1. N-KB3	P-Q4
2. P-KN3	N-QB3
3. P-Q4	B-N5
4. B-N2	Q-Q2
5. P-B4	PxP

Giving up the center is surely no better than 5. . . . P-K3 6. Q-N3 0-0-0. Now the skirmishing begins!

6. P-Q5!	BxN
7. BxB	N-K4
8. B-N2	0-0-0
9. Q-Q4!	N-QB3!
10. QxBP	P-K3!
11. N-B3	. . .

If 11. PxN, then Q-Q8 mate.

| 11. ... | N-N5 |
| 12. B-N5! | P-KB3?? |

Until now, a fierce war of nerves. Unfortunately, the prospect of material gain is too much for Black to resist. 12. ... N-KB3 would have continued the duel.

| 13. B-R3! | K-N1 |
| 14. BxKP | Q-K2 |

Looks like Black wins a piece or the exchange. The fact is he'll be a big pawn down.

| 15. 0-0!! | Q-B4 |

After 15. ... PxB, simply 16. BxN RxB? 17. P-Q6! winning the rook.

| 16. QxQ | BxQ |
| 17. B-B4 | ... |

And Black may resign a hopeless ending.

126. *Dutch Defense*

The case of the ill-considered pawn move. *When one advances a pawn, the pawn leaves behind a weakness that pieces alone must defend.* After all, a pawn does not move backwards.

| 1. N-KB3! | P-KB4?! |

Impervious to his opponent's play, Black willy-nilly essays his favorite defense.

2. P-K4!	PxP
3. N-N5	N-KB3
4. P-Q3!	PxP?

A greedy pawn-grab is violently punished.

| 5. BxP | P-K4 |

After ... P-KN3 6. P-KR4 P-Q4 7. P-R5, Black may resist longer, but the light squares weakness will eventually bring White victory.

| 6. NxP! | NxN |

White also wins after 6. ... RxN 7. BxR NxB 8. Q-R5+ K-K2 9. QxN, threatening B-N5+ winning the queen.

| 7. B-N6+! | K-K2 |
| 8. BxN! | RxB? |

Of course Black's position was already shattered.

| 9. B-N5+ |

Black loses his queen.

127. *Dutch Defense*

At any cost Black is determined to double White's queen bishop pawns. With this shallow plan firmly in mind, he misplaces his own king bishop, doubles his own king pawns, and finally falls for a beauty after neglecting to bring out his other bishop.

1.	P-QB4	P-KB4
2.	N-QB3	N-KB3
3.	P-KN3	P-K3
4.	B-N2	B-N5?

Correct is B-K2.

5.	Q-N3!	P-QR4
6.	N-B3	0-0
7.	0-0	K-R1
8.	P-Q4	N-K5?

Black ought to hold the center with P-Q4.

9.	NxN!	PxN
10.	B-N5!	Q-K1?

Better is 10. ... B-K2. No bargain barter is three pieces for the queen—if 10. ... PxN, then 11. BxQ PxB 12. KxP RxB 13. P-B5! N-B3 14. P-QR3 P-R5 15. Q-Q1 B-R4 16. QxP followed by P-QN4!

11.	N-Q2	N-B3
12.	P-Q5	BxN
13.	BxB	N-Q5
14.	Q-Q1	PxP
15.	B-QB3	N-B4
16.	QxP	R-R3
17.	QxKP	R-K3
18.	Q-Q3	RxP
19.	QR-K1	RxR
20.	RxR	Q-R4
21.	R-K4	N-Q3??

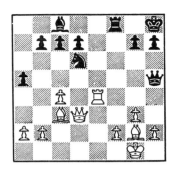

The queen bishop still does not play. It gets a chance after P-Q3.

22. R-R4!!	Resigns

After 22. . . . Q-KB4, 23. R-B4 wins the queen!

128. *Dutch Defense*

The dark squares go sour and the dark queen cannot be around to churn up a new batch.

1. N-KB3	P-KB4
2. P-KN3	P-Q3
3. P-Q4	P-KN3
4. B-N2	N-KB3
5. 0-0	B-N2
6. P-B4	P-B3
7. N-B3	0-0
8. Q-B2	N-R3
9. P-QR3	N-B2
10. R-K1	P-Q4?

A horrendous weakening of the dark squares. White could have essayed P-K4 on move nine. Why not allow him this dubious pleasure on move eleven? After 10. . . . K-R1 11. P-K4 PxP 12. NxP NxN 13. QxN, White would have strong pressure against a backward king pawn. However, Black may improve greatly with 12. . . . B-B4!

11. PxP!	PxP

Better is . . . N(2)xP.

12. B-B4	N-K3
13. B-K5	. . .

Complete domination of the dark squares is accomplished after the swap of the enemy king bishop.

13. . . .	N-K5?

Correct is P-N3 and B-N2.

14. P-K3	P-N3
15. BxB	KxB
16. N-K5	B-N2
17. QR-B1	NxN?

This permits a mere flank pawn, the QN pawn, to participate in the central action. More accurate is N(3)-N4-B2.

18. PxN!	Q-Q3
19. P-QB4	KR-B1

Routine and wrong; QR-N1, protecting the bishop, was necessary.

20. Q-N3	PxP

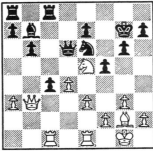

Unfortunately best.

21. NxBP	Q-B2
22. P-Q5!	N-N4
23. Q-N2+	K-R3

After ... K-N1 24. N-R5! Q-Q2 25. NxB QxN 26. P-Q6, White wins handily.

24. N-K5

There is no salvation: ... Q-N1 (Q3 or Q1) 25. P-KR4 N-K5 26. N-B7+ K-R4 27. B-B3 mate.

129. *Dutch Defense (Staunton Gambit)*

Some annotators criticize a move as inferior and then proceed to suggest an alternative just as bad. There are times when there is no better move. Then there are times—most—when there are better moves, but the commentator must labor to find them for the novice. Finally, there are times when even the novice must find the moves for himself, if he is to improve his game.

| 1. P-Q4 | P-KB4 |
| 2. P-K4!? | PxP |

The Staunton Gambit offers great possibilities for instant success, but no guarantees. White gives a pawn for fast development. When the attack mounts, he hopes the pressure will be too much for his rival. There is no point in refusing the gambit. Generally, the break at K4 is advantageous for White; so Black should charge something for the privilege.

| 3. N-QB3 | N-KB3 |
| 4. B-KN5 | P-B3 |

The other choices are no less complicated: N-QB3, P-QN3, P-K3, or P-KN3.

| 5. P-B3 | PxP |

If Black is willing to suffer, he may take this pawn in order to play for the win.

6. NxP	P-K3
7. B-Q3	P-Q3
8. 0-0	B-K2
9. N-KR4	QN-Q2

No need to say White threatened 10. BxN, followed by Q-R5+.

| 10. N-K4 | 0-0 |
| 11. NxN | PxN? |

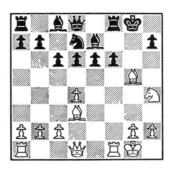

After 11. ... NxN, White may try 12. N-N6, but the win would be far from view.

| 12. BxP+! | KxB |

Whatever happens, Q-R5 is coming.

13. Q-R5+	K-N1
14. Q-N6+	K-R1
15. N-B5!!	...

Now the king rook file is open for business.

| 15. ... | PxN |
| 16. R-B3 | |

And there can be no improvement on checkmate.

130. *Dutch Defense*

A lone knight can and often does ably defend his king. Posted at KB3, the knight remains vigilant, for he knows that the king can never be left completely alone. Thus, to destroy the knight at KB3 is a common objective, and when he falls, the king must submit.

1. P-Q4	P-KB4

This order of moves allows the Staunton Gambit—2. P-K4. The other order, 1. ... P-K3 and 2. ... P-KB4, can transpose into the French Defense after 2. P-K4. Take your choice!

2. P-QB4	N-KB3
3. N-QB3	P-K3
4. P-K3	P-QN3!

Hindering White's plan: B-Q3, KN-K2, P-B3 and P-K4.

5. B-Q3	B-N2
6. N-B3	B-K2
7. 0-0	0-0
8. Q-B2	P-B4
9. PxP?!	. . .

This careless exchange permits Black more effectively to post his king bishop for the attack.

9. ...	BxP
10. P-K4?	. . .

Better is P-QR3 with a view toward expanding on the queen side and posting the bishop on QN2. White's last advance leaves a gaping hole on Q4 for the enemy minor pieces and further increases the agility of Black's king bishop.

10. ...	N-B3
11. P-QR3	Q-N1!
12. PxP	. . .

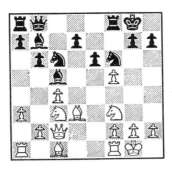

Safer is P-R3. The win of the pawn is illusory.

| 12. ... | N-KN5! |

The winning move. The best White can do to prolong the struggle is to play: 13. P-KN3 N(3)-K4 14. NxN NxN 15. B-K2 RxP and White is busted positionally—but he's not mated yet!

13. N-K2	N-Q5
14. N(2)xN	KBxN
15. P-R3?	...

The last hope in a bad position was 15. B-K4 RxP 16. P-R3(!). Hoping to dispatch the knight without delay, White falls into the net.

| 15. ... | BxN! |
| 16. PxN | Q-N6!! |

Again the pin, this time on the king bishop pawn, forecloses on White's game with checkmate.

131. *Dutch Defense*

Aggressive play induces the blunder!

| 1. P-Q4 | P-KB4 |
| 2. N-QB3 | ... |

An unusual treatment of the Dutch, but quite acceptable. The idea is to achieve a rapid break at K4, possible because Black has already weakened his king position by 1. . . . P-KB4.

| 2. . . . | N-KB3 |
| 3. B-N5 | N-K5?! |

Moving a piece twice in the early stages of the opening? Better is 3. . . . P-KN3.

| 4. NxN | PxN |
| 5. P-KB3! | . . . |

In order to eliminate the blockading king pawn.

5. . . .	P-Q4
6. P-K3	B-B4
7. PxP	BxP
8. N-K2!	P-KR3?

Driving the bishop to a better spot and further weakening the king position. 8. . . . Q-Q3 is an improvement.

9. B-B4	N-B3
10. N-B3	B-N3
11. B-Q3	B-B2

Black must retain his bishop to defend the light squares.

| 12. 0-0 | P-K4? |

Caesar was ambitious. With a temporary pawn sacrifice, Black hopes to weaken White's configuration and castle long, ready for a king side attack. Correct is 12. . . . P-K3 and then B-Q3.

| 13. PxP! | Q-Q2 |
| 14. P-K6!! | . . . |

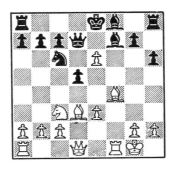

White returns the temporary sac with a vengeance!

14. ...   **QxP?**

The greater of two evils; the lesser evil being 14. ... BxP
15. Q-R5+ K-Q1 16. QR-Q1(!).

    15. N-N5!

Black loses at least the exchange!

132. *Dutch Defense In Reverse*

White sets a trap or two and wins a pawn by accurate play.
He avoids an enemy snare and then speeds Black's demise by
using the lead pawn as the bait!

1. P-KN3	P-Q4
2. P-KB4	P-KN3
3. N-KB3	B-N2
4. B-N2	P-QB4
5. 0-0	N-QB3
6. N-B3	N-B3
7. P-Q3	P-Q5

Black would like to establish an outpost on K6.

8. N-QR4	N-Q2
9. P-B4	P-QR3
10. B-Q2	0-0

First trap. If 10. . . . P-QN4, then 11. PxP PxP 12. NxBP! NxN
13. Q-B2, regaining the piece with a fine game.

11.	Q-B2	Q-B2
12.	P-QR3	P-N3
13.	P-QN4	B-N2
14.	QR-N1	N-Q1
15.	PxP	PxP
16.	N-N6!!	R-N1

Another trap. If 16. . . . NxN, then 17. B-R5! and White's
superiority is increased.

17.	NxN	QxN
18.	R-N6	Q-B2
19.	R(1)-N1	N-B3
20.	Q-N2!	B-R1
21.	N-N5!	KR-B1

Trying to defend his queen bishop pawn.

| 22. | N-K4 | Q-R2 |

Now Black sets the trap! If 23. NxP, then RxR 24. QxR
R-N1 25. QxQ RxR (with check!) and it is Black who wins!

23.	K-B2!!	B-B1
24.	NxP	P-K3
25.	NxRP	BxP?

Black is two pawns down; he wants one of them back. Now he loses quickly.

| 26. Q-N3 | RxR |
| 27. QxR | Q-K2?? |

Exchange queens with a pawn down? Never!

| 28. P-B5!! | Resigns. |

White leisurely wins the bishop at R3.

133. *English Opening*

Pressing a routine attack against the Black pawn base (QB3), White employs a pin from which he himself has no retreat.

1. P-QB4	P-KN3
2. N-QB3	B-N2
3. P-KN3	P-K4
4. B-N2	P-Q3
5. P-Q3	P-KB4
6. P-K3	N-KB3
7. KN-K2	0-0
8. 0-0	P-B3
9. P-QN4	B-K3
10. P-N5	Q-B2!

Seemingly begging for mercy, but actually setting the snare.

11. PxP	PxP
12. N-N5?!	Q-Q2
13. B-R3	N-K1
14. R-N1?	. . .

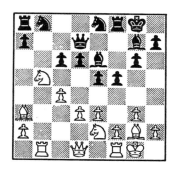

White is in over his head. He should have played 14. B-N2
P-B5?! 15. KPxP PxP 16. BxB KxB 17. N(2)-Q4!

| 14. ... | **P-B5!** |
| **15. KPxP** | ... |

Slightly better is N-B1.

| 15. ... | **PxP** |
| **16. NxBP** | ... |

There is no choice. After 16. KN-B3 B-N5 17. P-B3 B-B4,
the knight on QN5 has no retreat.

16. ...	**RxN**
17. PxR	**P-QR3!**
18. P-KB5	**BxKBP**
19. NxP	**NxN**
20. R-K1	**B-B3**

And Black brings his material edge to fruition thus: 21.
BxN QxB 22. R-K8+ K-B2 23. Q-K1 Q-B2 24. R-N3 P-QR4
25. P-Q4 B-Q2 26. R-K2 N-R3 27. R-KB3 B-N5 28. RxB+
KxR 29. P-B3 B-B4 30. Q-R4+ P-N4 31. Q-R6+ B-N3 32. R-K5
K-B2 33. QxP N-N5 34. B-R3 Q-Q3 35. Q-B4+ K-N2 36. Q-K3
N-B7 37. R-K7+ K-B1 and the rest is history.

134. *English Opening*

Remember the old Three Knights Game? 1. P-K4 P-K4 2. N-KB3 N-QB3 3. N-B3. ... This early, White sets a snare. He hopes Black will make the *natural* developing move. 3. ... B-B4? 4. NxP! BxP+ 5. KxB NxN 6. P-Q4 and white's enormous center and the bishop pair far outweigh his inability to castle. Now we shall see an old theme in modern verse!

1.	P-QB4	N-KB3
2.	N-QB3	P-K4
3.	N-B3	N-B3
4.	P-KN3	B-B4?

Black is too anxious to gain the initiative.

5.	NxP!	BxP+
6.	KxB	NxN
7.	P-K4	P-B4

Black must hold back White's central pawn mass.

8.	P-Q3	P-Q3
9.	P-KR3	P-KR4

Better to save time with B-K3.

10.	B-K2	N-R2
11.	K-N2	P-R5
12.	P-KN4	N-N4
13.	B-K3	B-Q2
14.	Q-Q2	N-K3
15.	P-N4!	. . .

With greater mobility White does not fear to operate on both wings.

15.	. . .	P-QN3
16.	QR-N1	B-B3
17.	KR-KB1	B-N2

18. K-N1	N-B3
19. N-Q5	N(B)-Q5
20. B-Q1	P-B3
21. K-R2	B-B3
22. P-R4!	P-R4
23. PxRP	PxP
24. Q-KB2	R-QR2
25. P-N5!	0-0

Not very appetizing, but after 25. . . . PxP there follows 26. BxN PxB 27. Q-B5! (26. . . . NxB is answered by 27. B-R5+!).

| 26. P-N6! | P-B4 |

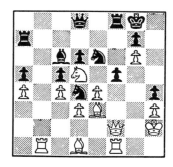

| 27. R-N8!! | Resigns. |

The queen is lost. After 27. . . . QxR, 28. QxRP and mate cannot be avoided.

135. *English Opening*

A pin, a fork, and suddenly the end.

1. P-QB4	P-K4
2. N-QB3	N-KB3
3. N-B3	N-B3
4. P-KN3	B-N5?!

Either P-Q3 or P-Q4 is fine. The text is a waste of time and misplaces the bishop to boot.

5. N-Q5!   NxN?

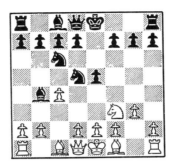

Bring back the bishop to K2!

6. PxN   **P-K5??**

After 6. .... N-K2 7. NxP NxP 8. Q-N3 P-QB3 9. B-N2 Q-K2 10. BxN, White does win a pawn, but that is the lesser evil.

7. PxN!	**PxN**
8. Q-N3!!	**Q-K2**
9. P-QR3!	

If the bishop moves, PxNP forks the rook and the other bishop, winning a piece.

136. *English Opening*

A routine pin-breaking simplification.

1.	P-QB4	P-K4
2.	N-KB3	N-QB3
3.	N-B3	N-B3
4.	P-Q4	PxP
5.	NxP	B-N5
6.	B-N5	P-KR3

Black wants the queen bishop to retreat so that it will be unable to interfere with a check by interposing at Q2.

7. B-R4!   **N-K5??**

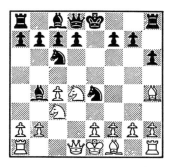

Exhilarated with the prospect of 8. BxQ NxN(6) 9. PxN BxP+; or 9. Q-Q3 N-K5+; or 9. Q-B2 NxN recovering the queen with a won game. But Black has unwittingly sipped the hemlock.

8. BxQ	**NxN(6)**
9. NxN!!	**NxQ+**
10. NxB!	

And it is White who is exhilarated.

137. *English Opening*

The English formation often entices Black into the impetuous advance P-K5. The very best Black can expect is the exchange of his more valuable central pawn for a flank pawn—in this case 6. P-KN4!, after which he must be prepared to defend the worse game.

1. P-QB4	**P-K4**
2. N-QB3	**N-KB3**
3. N-B3	**P-Q3**
4. P-Q4	**P-K5?!**

Black should curtail his ambitions with QN-Q2.

5. N-KN5	B-B4
6. P-KN4!	BxP
7. B-N2	N-B3

Naturally White must regain his pawn, and in view of this, Black should prepare to block the long White diagonal with P-B3.

8. N(N)xKP	NxN

Better is B-K2.

9. NxN	Q-Q2
10. P-KR3!	B-B4
11. N-N3	B-N3
12. P-KR4	P-KR3
13. Q-N3!	. . .

After this, life becomes miserable on the White squares. Under pressure, Black snatches the lonely pawn; he should continue either with 13. ... 0-0-0 or 13. R-QN1 followed by B-K2 and castles.

13. ...	NxP?
14. Q-K3!+	. . .

The point is that White doesn't want the knight pawn—yet!

14. ...	N-K3
15. P-B4	P-KB4
16. BxP	. . .

223

The collapse on the White squares costs Black a piece.

16. ...	R-QN1
17. B-B6!	QxB
18. QxN+	

And there goes the piece!

138. *English Opening*

Veiled disaster visits the pawn-grabber.

1. P-QB4	N-KB3
2. N-QB3	P-K4
3. P-KN3	P-B3
4. P-Q4	...

Preferable is 4. N-B3.

4. ...	PxP
5. QxP	P-Q4
6. N-B3	B-K2
7. B-N2	0-0
8. 0-0	P-B4
9. Q-Q3	P-Q5?!

A futile attempt to wrest the initiative from a better organized adversary; 9. ... PxP 10. QxP N-B3 leads to even chances.

10. N-Q5!   ...

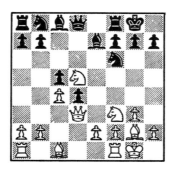

"Now is the hour. I'm only slightly better after 10. . . . N-B3 11. P-K4! PxPe.p. 12. BxP. Perhaps Black will nibble on a pawn!"

10. ...	NxN?!
11. PxN	QxP??
12. N-N5!!	

The White bishop is unsheathed, while in concert the queen and knight menace mate. There is no defense.

139. *English Opening*

After resigning, someone once remarked to his victorious grandmaster opponent: "You're no grandmaster; you just wait for a blunder!" If that's how to win, then wait! You'll be a grandmaster if you know just how long to wait.

1. P-QB4	P-K4
2. N-QB3	N-KB3
3. P-KN3	P-B3
4. N-B3	P-K5
5. N-Q4	P-Q4
6. PxP	Q-N3
7. N-N3	PxP
8. B-N2	B-KB4
9. P-Q3!	. . .

White could not castle because of P-Q5. But castling takes a back seat when one has the chance to crack the enemy's center.

9. ...	PxP
10. 0-0!!	. . .

The point! White has a strong attack with the option of recovering the pawn: 10. . . . PxP 11. QxP+.

10. ...	N-B3
11. B-N5!	0-0-0

Consider well! There is more terrain to defend in castling queen side.

| 12. PxP | B-K3 |
| 13. R-B1 | ... |

We shall soon see why White keeps his queen bishop rather than play BxN weakening Black's pawns.

13. ...	K-N1
14. P-Q4	B-K2
15. N-R4	Q-B2
16. N3/-B5!	P-KR3
17. B-K3!!	...

A quiet waiting move! White could have played the aggressive B-B4, but with no effect.

| 17. ... | R-QB1?? |

N-KN5 offers more resistance. Now White strikes the decisive blow as Black cannot protect both Q3 and QN2.

| 18. B-B4! | ... |

Back to haunt Black.

| 18. ... | B-Q3 |
| 19. Q-N3!! | Resigns. |

The double threat cannot be met: 20. BxB QxB 21. QxP mate; and 20. N-R6+ winning the queen.

226

140. *English Opening*

For over a decade White has employed a system which necessarily involves an early weakening of the white squares on the queen side, notably Q3. The weaknesses were thought to be temporary. White would customarily expand his pawn center, thereby fatally cramping Black's game. Here Black explodes with an early pawn sacrifice and sudden retribution visits his rival on those very White squares!

1. P-QB4	P-K4
2. N-QB3	N-QB3
3. P-KN3	B-B4
4. B-N2	N-B3
5. P-K3	. . .

Why not the simple N-B3 and 0-0? After all, P-K3 may be essayed at a later stage with good effect.

5. . . .	P-Q4!

This is the new move gnawing at White's presumed advantage. Other moves, such as 0-0 and P-Q3, allow KN-K2 and a strong P-Q4.

6. NxP	NxN
7. PxN	. . .

Or 7. BxN N-N5 8. B-K4 P-B4 with good play for the pawn.

7. . . .	N-N5
8. Q-N3	P-QB3!

Black must follow through. White, of course, may be less obstinate and return the pawn with P-QR3.

9. PxP	PxP
10. P-Q4?!	. . .

Playing right into Black's hands. White should have considered 10. P-QR3 N-Q6+ 11. K-K2 NxB+ (BxP+ was threatened!) 12. RxN etc. Of course, Black does have an im-

provement: 11. ... B-N5+ 12. P-B3 B-B4 13. P-K4 NxB+
14. RxN B-Q2 with minimal compensation for the pawn.

| 10. ... | PxP |
| 11. PxP | B-KB4 |

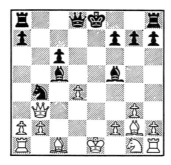

White has sailed into the soup, if that's possible! The sticky
point is that after Black checks on QB7, he captures the rook
with tempo on the queen. Else, White might have time to
regroup.

| 12. BxP+ | ... |

Taking the bishop leads to mate or the loss of the queen.

12. ...	K-B1!
13. K-B1	NxB
14. PxB	N-Q5
15. Q-Q1	B-B7

Also decisive is N-B7.

16. Q-Q2	Q-Q4
17. P-B3	R-K1
18. P-QN4	R-K7!

If 19. NxR, then QxP+ ends the battle.

141. *English Opening*

In most queen-pawn-type positions White allows his QB pawn to be captured in order to lure an enemy central pawn off course. Usually the pawn is conveniently recovered. Relying on the usual, White is conveniently snared.

1. P-QB4	N-KB3
2. N-QB3	P-K3
3. N-B3	B-N5
4. P-KN3	. . .

The fianchetto isn't always aptly modern. Simple and good is Q-B2 followed by P-QR3.

4. . . .	0-0
5. B-N2	P-Q4
6. 0-0?	. . .

The refutation of the text is remarkable. 6. P-QR3(!) would have been better, since Black cannot permanently double White's pawns with BxN, i.e. White stands prepared to swap off his pawn on QB4.

6. . . .	PxP!
7. Q-R4	. . .

White wants his money back. If 7. N-K5, Q-Q5 holds the pawn.

7. . . .	N-R3
8. P-QR3	B-Q2!
9. N-QN5?	. . .

One should not throw good money after bad. The pawn is gone. Why compound matters by walking into the pin? There is the simple 9. Q-B2 BxN 10. QxB B-B3 (10. . . . P-QN4 11. P-QR4!) with equality.

9. . . .	Q-K1
10. N(3)-Q4?	. . .

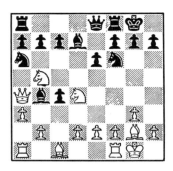

The knights are tripping over themselves while the other pieces lay dormant. Although not very appetizing in itself, the last chance is 10. NxBP! BxQ 11. NxQ B-K2 12. NxN+ BxN when White's queen side is slightly paralyzed; yet he is alive!

10. ...	**P-K4!**
11. **BxP**	**PxN**
12. **BxN**	...

After 12. QxN, BxN wins the queen.

12. ...	**B-R6!!**

With no pieces left to defend the king, this sudden incursion decides.

13. **PxB**	...

Mate ensues after 13. QxB QxP! Also futile is 13. Q-Q1 Q-B3 14. P-B3 B-Q3 and the bishop on QR6 is doomed.

13. ...	**Q-K5!**

White intended to defend against 13. ... QxP with 14. Q-Q1. Black cleverly creates a situation in which mate will be menaced when he captures the king pawn. In order to divert the Black queen, White's next is forced.

14. **B-N7**	**QxB**
15. **P-B3**	**B-Q2**

The final poetry; the horse is stunned by the pin.

142. *English Opening*

1. N-KB3	P-Q4
2. P-KN3	N-KB3
3. B-N2	P-K3
4. 0-0	B-K2
5. P-B4	PxP
6. Q-R4+	QN-Q2
7. QxBP	P-QR3
8. Q-B2	0-0
9. N-B3	P-B3?

Black is bluffed out of the aggressive P-B4 if only because he thinks he can clog up White's king bishop. But his own bishop, as a result, remains hemmed in by its own pawns.

10. P-N3	Q-B2
11. B-N2	P-QN4
12. N-K4	NxN
13. QxN	B-N2
14. N-K5!	N-B3

To escape a cramped position one naturally prepares the crucial break. By normal development White anticipates this break and cleverly refutes it. If 14. ... B-B3 then 15. NxN!

15. Q-B3!	N-Q4?

White has kept up the pressure along the long diagonal. Black should therefore defend his pieces stationed on that line: R-QN1!

16. P-Q4	P-QB4??

The ill-prepared break!

17. KR-B1	B-Q3
18. P-K4!	N-B3
19. Q-K2	Q-N3
20. N-Q3!	N-Q2
21. PxP	NxP

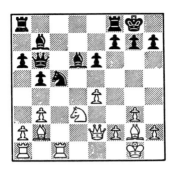

22. B-Q4!   . . .

The pin cannot be broken; P-QN4 will now be fatal for Black.

22. . . .   **Resigns.**

143. *English Opening*

As a youngster, Lombardy produced this absurdity: 1. P-KN3 P-QN3 2. B-N2 B-N2 3. BxB. . . . Considerable thought offered the equation. "If he can do it, why can't I?" So. . . . 3. . . . P-KN3 4. P-QN3 B-N2! 5. B-N2! BxB and after the mutual exchange of rooks and bishops, Black won! Such are the dangers in the fianchetto development!

1. P-QB4	N-KB3
2. N-KB3	P-KN3
3. P-QN3	B-N2
4. B-N2	0-0
5. P-N3	P-Q3
6. B-N2	P-K4
7. 0-0	N-R4!

Ostensibly, Black intends P-KB4 and king side action.

8. P-Q3?	. . .

Actually he has set a little trap. More logical is 8. N-B3 P-KB4 9. P-K3 P-KN4 10. N-K1 P-N5 11. P-B3 N-KB3 12. P-B4! with an edge for White.

| 8. ... | P-K5! |

If 9. N-Q4, P-QB4 still nets a piece.

9. BxB	PxN
10. BxR	PxB
11. KxP	QxB

And White has insufficient compensation for the loss of two pieces for a rook.

144. *English Opening*

Premature flank attack: Often a player may jockey for position, wait for his opponent to castle and then spring a decisive attack. Here such a plan is a luxury.

1. P-QB4	P-Q3
2. N-QB3	P-KN3
3. P-KN3	B-N2
4. B-N2	P-K4
5. P-Q3	N-K2
6. P-K4	0-0
7. P-KR4?	...

Normal development, please (7. KN-K2)!

7. ...	N-Q2
8. P-R5	N-KB3!
9. PxP	BPxP!

The only significant lines belong to Black for the king bishop file towers over the king rook file.

10. B-N5	P-B3
11. Q-Q2	R-B2
12. P-B4	...

The royal flight to the queen side (0-0-0) is still possible.

12. ...	B-N5
13. KN-K2	P-QN4!
14. PxNP	PxNP

After 15. NxP Q-N3 16. N(5)-B3 R-N1, White cannot hope to castle anywhere.

15. P-B5	P-N5!
16. PxP	PxP
17. N-Q5	N(B)xN
18. PxN	Q-Q2
19. B-K4	N-B4
20. 0-0-0	...

The king side is lost; so off to the other wing!

| 20. ... | P-N6! |

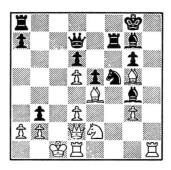

The ultimate stroke prying open the position.

21. PxP	BxN
22. QxB	N-Q5
23. Q-R2	NxP+
24. K-N1	Q-R4
25. B-K7	Q-R8+
26. K-B2	N-Q5+
27. K-Q2	B-R3+
28. K-K1	. . .

If 28. QxB, then . . . QxP+ and mates.

| 28. . . . | Q-R4+ |

White must lose a whole rook.

145. *English Opening*

To all appearances Black has the initiative. In an effort to defend the queen side White's king knight is forced to scurry about, holding the position intact. At last Black is *successful.* He gets his booty, only to be confronted by that tireless and somewhat deadly knight.

1. P-QB4	P-QB4
2. N-QB3	N-QB3
3. N-B3	N-B3
4. P-Q4	PxP
5. NxP	P-K3

The fianchetto of the king bishop in this position at one time was considered suspect but is actually quite playable, even against the Maroczy Bind (6. P-K4) which attempts to impede Black's central break (P-Q4).

| 6. P-KN3 | . . . |

Now 6. P-K4 is met by . . . B-N5.

6. . . .	Q-N3
7. P-K3	B-N5
8. B-N2	N-K4?!

8. . . . P-Q4 equalizes.

9. Q-N3	Q-B4
10. N-B2	B-R4?!

White gets adequate compensation for the pawn after
10. . . . BxN+ 11. QxB QxP 12. QxN QxN 13. B-Q2 0-0 14.
B-N4 R-K1 15. B-Q6(!).

11. N-R3	P-Q4

11. . . . N-Q6+ 12. K-K2 NxB+ 13. QRxN only facilitates
White's plans for rapid development.

12. PxP	NxP
13. 0-0!	NxN
14. PxN	QxBP?

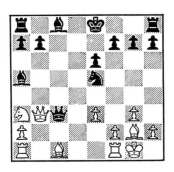

Black has seen all, except the truth. Instead of biting on the
pawn, Black should continue with 14. . . . 0-0 15. N-N5
N-B5(!) with good play.

15. N-N5!	QxQ

If 15. . . . QxR, 16. B-QR3 N-B6+ 17. BxN Q-B3 18. N-Q6+,
etc.

16. PxQ	B-N3
17. B-R3	P-QR3
18. N-Q6+	K-Q2
19. KR-Q1	K-B2
20. N-N5+!	

White wins too much: 20. ... PxN 21. B-Q6+ K-Q1 22. BxN+ K-K1 23. RxR.

146. *English Opening*

Confusion is a formidable foe. Black gives up a pawn, thinking he will regain the material under favorable circumstances with the occupation by his knight of the vital QB4 square. Failing this, he becomes jittery, and subsequently he falls into a one-mover!

1. P-QB4	P-QB4
2. N-QB3	N-QB3
3. P-K3	P-KN3
4. P-Q4	B-N2
5. N-B3	P-Q3
6. B-K2	N-R3?!

'A knight on the side one cannot abide,' goes the adage. The text can be recommended only if there were a previously weakened square at Q5 where the knight may rest his weary bones. The White pawn stationed at K3 therefore negates the knight move.

7. P-Q5!	N-K4
8. NxN	PxN?!

Rather than permanently ruin the pawn structure, Black should adopt the following course: 8. ... BxN 9. P-K4 B-N2 10. B-K3 P-K4. Although Black has lost valuable time, he retains good practical chances.

9. P-K4	P-B3
10. P-QR3	N-B2
11. P-QN4!!	B-R3?

To exchange a bishop hindered by its own pawns is in itself a fine idea, but the timing is off. Black should castle. Then he answers 12. PxP with Q-R4 without fear of Q-R4+.

12. BxB	NxB
13. PxP!	0-0
14. Q-N3	N-B2
15. 0-0	Q-B2
16. Q-N4	K-N2?!

In an inferior position, practical chances are often offered by the sacrifice of the exchange: 16. ... B-Q2 17. N-N5 Q-B1—keeping an eye on the bishop pawn, 18. P-Q6 BxN 19. PxP B-B3 20. PxR=Q+ QxQ etc.

17. N-N5!	Q-Q1
18. P-Q6	B-Q2??

Threatening BxN and then PxP, knocking out the queen pawn. Too bad, but there's no time; 18. ... PxP was forced.

19. P-B6!!

After 19. ... BxP, 20. PxP forks the queen and rook.

147. *English Opening*

If White can break open the center with P-K4 he gains an enormous advantage in space. He suffers under the illusion that Black must give up a bishop for a knight to prevent the break. Only after the move does he discover how wrong he was!

1. P-Q4	N-KB3
2. P-QB4	P-B4

3. KN-B3	PxP
4. NxP	P-K3
5. N-QB3	B-N5
6. P-K3	0-0
7. B-Q3	P-Q4
8. 0-0	N-B3
9. NxN?	PxN

Because he thinks he will break with P-K4, White strengthens Black's center by this frivolous exchange.

10. P-QR3   **B-Q3**

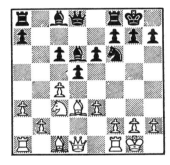

The bishop calmly retreats.

| 11. P-K4? | NxP! |
| 12. NxN | PxN |

Suddenly the grim truth; if 13. BxP then BxP+ 14. KxB Q-R5+ regaining the bishop and remaining a pawn up.

13. B-B2	P-KB4
14. Q-K2	P-QR4
15. B-Q2	Q-B2
16. P-KN3	P-B4
17. QR-N1	B-N2
18. B-B3	B-K4
19. P-B3?!	. . .

White's desperation to regain his pawn allows Black a neat finish.

19. ...	BxB
20. PxB	PxP!
21. QxP+	K-R1
22. Q-QN6	QxQ
23. RxQ	B-K5!

Gaining needed time to protect the pawn edge.

24. B-Q1	B-Q6
25. RxP	BxP
26. R-K3	QR-Q1
27. B-K2	B-R7

The bishops must not be exchanged—yet!

28. R-K7	B-Q4
29. R-QR6	P-KB5
30. R(6)-R7	P-B6
31. RxNP	B-K5!!

The rooks on the 7th are too late. Black's pawn nets a piece and the game. White resigns.

148. *Grünfeld Defense*

A quiet developing move lulls White into a false sense of security. He wastes time defending his bulky pawn center, the roof never fell in so fast!

1. P-QB4	N-KB3
2. P-Q4	P-KN3
3. N-QB3	P-Q4
4. PxP	NxP
5. P-K4	NxN
6. PxN	B-N2
7. B-QB4	P-QB4
8. N-K2	N-B3
9. B-K3	0-0
10. P-KR4	...

One observes that White developed his pieces with a view to defending his pawn center while Black concentrated on applying pressure on that center. Having achieved central stability, White feels ambitious enough to organize a kingside onslaught, a good enough plan in itself, if one remains alert to the dangers.

10. ...	PxP
11. PxP	Q-Q3!

Threatening to win a piece with Q-N5+.

12. R-QB1	R-Q1
13. P-Q5?!	...

Preferable was P-K5 obstructing Black's king bishop.

13. ...	N-K4
14. Q-N3?!	...

If White really wants to play P-B3, now is the time.

14. ...	B-Q2!!

Never did a winning move look so harmless.

15. P-B3?	P-QN4
16. B-Q3	...

White is lost anyway, but there is absolutely no struggle after his last move. For those who prefer to fight on with some material compensation for a lost piece we recommend the fol-

lowing: 16. BxNP QR-N1! 17. P-R4 P-QR3 18. B-B5 Q-KB3
19. Q-R3. White may positively state that you can't win by
resigning!

16. ...   Q-N5+!!

Resigns. After QxQ Black plays NxB+, recovering the queen
with a piece ahead; or after K-B1 Black exchanges queens
and captures the bishop on Q3 anyway.

149. *Grünfeld Defense*

The continuing saga of the queen knight pawn.

1. P-Q4	N-KB3
2. P-QB4	P-KN3
3. N-QB3	P-Q4
4. Q-N3	PxP
5. QxBP	B-K3

The notion of gaining time by attacking the queen is a
paradox, for here the lady can be driven to a better square.
But maybe White will err!

6. Q-N5+?   ...

Always check, it might be mate; 6. Q-Q3 favors White.

6. ...   N-B3

If 7. Qx the knight pawn (?), NxP!

7. N-B3   N-Q4!

Stopping to defend the knight pawn asks for trouble, for
P-K4 would be played anyway.

8. P-K4   ...

Not 8. QxP N(4)-N5!

8. ...	P-QR3!
9. Q-N3?	...

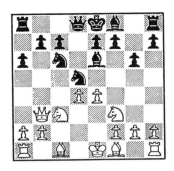

The only move is 9. Q-K2, for if instead 9. Q-Q3, then N(4)-N5 10. Q-Q1 NxQP! 11. NxN QxN! 12. QxQ N-B7+ 13. K-Q1 NxQ wins a pawn.

9. ...	**N-K6!**
10. N-Q5	...

If 10. P-Q5, then N-R4 11. Q-R4+ B-Q2 12. QxN P-N3 13. Q-R3 N-B7+ catches the dame.

10. ...	**NxN**
11. PxN	**QxP**
12. QxP	...

Taking the queen knight pawn begs for a speedy execution as a remedy for a lost position. White is already a pawn minus, on top of being saddled with a weak isolated queen pawn.

12. ...	**Q-K5+**

Check first cuts off the retreat of the queen as now QN3 is covered by the queen bishop.

13. B-K3	...

We may examine another futile try: 13. K-Q1 R-R2 14. N-Q2 Q-Q4 14. Q-N3 Q-R4+ 15. Q-B3 B-N5 pinning and winning.

13. ...	**R-R2!!**

and a piece goes.

150. *Grünfeld Defense*

Black overextends himself—he comes forward too quickly with too much for too little in return.

1. P-Q4	N-KB3
2. N-KB3	P-KN3
3. P-KN3	B-N2
4. B-N2	0-0
5. 0-0	P-Q4
6. P-B4	PxP
7. Q-R4	N-B3
8. R-Q1	N-Q2
9. QxBP	N-N3

The queen is buffeted about, but White's preponderance in the center easily holds the attack at bay.

10. Q-N3	P-QR4
11. N-B3	P-R5
12. Q-B2	B-B4
13. Q-Q2!	...

Not 13. P-K4 B-N5 14. P-Q5 BxN 15. BxB N-Q5! with equality.

13. ...	N-B5
14. Q-B4	B-B7?

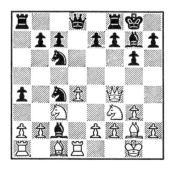

Delirious from the thrill of the chase, Black prods once more, only to find his position, as a result, completely overextended. The right way was: 14. ... Q-B1 15. P-K4 B-R6 (15. P-Q5 N(3)-K4!).

| 15. P-Q5!! | P-QN4 |

If 15. ... BxR, 16. QxN and White wins either the bishop or the knight.

| 16. NxNP | BxR |
| 17. QxN | P-R6 |

Hoping to create a diversion to save the bishop on Q8.

18. N-B3	N-R4
19. Q-Q3	B-N6
20. N-Q2!	. . .

Not 20. PxB NxP 21. R-N1 P-R7 etc.

20. . . .	R-N1
21. PxB	PxP
22. BxP	NxP
23. R-R2	P-QB3
24. NxN	RxN
25. Q-B2	Q-N3
26. PxP	P-K3
27. N-R4	Q-N5
28. P-R4	R-B1
29. BxB	KxB
30. Q-Q2	Q-N4
31. Q-Q4+	K-N1
32. R-N2	RxR
33. NxR	P-K4
34. Q-Q2	

White has a winning material advantage.

151. Grünfeld Defense

The blunder comes easy when you know how—and everyone knows how.

1. P-Q4	N-KB3
2. P-QB4	P-KN3
3. N-QB3	P-Q4
4. N-B3	B-N2
5. PxP	NxP
6. B-Q2	...

In vogue for its solid character. The plan is to preserve the strongpoint Q4 by preventing both Black's freeing moves ... P-K4 and ... P-QB4—a tall order.

6. ...	0-0
7. R-B1	N-N3

Mesmerized by the countless examples of this line in current tournament play, Black expects the tried 8. P-K3?! But the appraisal of a move must change with the advance of theoretical knowledge. Sharp but equal play results after 8. P-K3?! N(1)-Q2 9. B-K2 P-K4 10. 0-0 P-QB3 11. P-QN4 R-K1 12. P-QR4 P-K5! But. . . .

8. B-N5!	...

Lacking space and lagging behind in development, Black can hardly afford to ignore a sacred principle, *moving a piece twice in the opening.* Conversely, White may, at times, because of the initiative afforded by the first move, take such a liberty. The text is certainly more logical than 8. P-K3, which shuts in the bishop.

8. ...	P-KR3
9. B-R4	N-B3
10. P-K3	P-N4
11. B-N3	P-N5

An improvement: 11. ... B-N5 12. B-K2 P-K3 13. 0-0 Q-K2.

246

12. N-KR4!	P-K4
13. PxP	NxP
14. Q-B2	Q-N4
15. B-K2	P-KB4

Clearly ... P-QB3 was called for.

16. N-N5!	P-B3
17. N-Q6	N-Q4
18. 0-0	P-B5

Things are seldom what they seem—so with the strength of Black's attack.

| 19. PxP | NxP |
| 20. KR-K1 | B-K3 |

Hoping for 21. NxP B-Q4 with some attacking chances. Or 21. NxP QR-N1 22. N-B5 RxP! 23. QxR? N-B6+ winning the queen!

| 21. B-B1 | QR-Q1 |
| 22. QR-Q1 | ... |

Or 22. NxP?! R-Q7! 23. QxR? N-R6+ winning the queen.

| 22. ... | R-Q2 |
| 23. N-K4! | ... |

Black's game is not much worse, but. . . .

| 23. ... | RxR?? |
| 24. NxQ | |

Black thought he was getting two rooks for the queen but, owing to the mating threat, he can only get two knights, not enough!

152. *King's Indian Defense*

After the exchange of queens the game transposes into an Old Indian Defense in which Black hopes to accrue small positional advantages to compensate for the lag in development. As we shall see, there can be certain obstacles to such a plan.

1. P-Q4	N-KB3
2. P-QB4	P-KN3
3. N-QB3	B-N2
4. P-K4	P-Q3
5. B-K2	...

Watch out, fans! There is nothing blocking the action of White's king bishop pawn, which can still be used to pry open the center. The idea is quite new.

5. ...	P-K4?!
6. PxP!	PxP
7. QxQ+	KxQ
8. P-B4!!	...

Undermining the king pawn so that Black will be unable to post a knight at Q5. The activity of the White pieces is also enhanced tremendously.

| 8. ... | KN-Q2 |
| 9. N-B3 | P-KR3 |

Precautions must be taken to freeze out the White knights.

10. 0-0	N-QB3
11. B-K3	N-Q5
12. QR-Q1	NxB+

Why not swap knights? The bishop at K2 does no harm.

13. NxN	PxP
14. BxBP	R-K1
15. P-K5	P-QB3

Black had to weaken Q3 or leave Q4 unguarded.

16. N-B3	K-K2
17. N-K4	P-KN4
18. B-N3	P-N5??

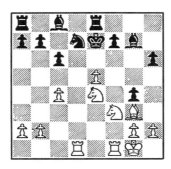

To adopt this opening great patience is demanded; instead the defender breaks under the strain.

| 19. N-R4 | NxP |
| 20. N-Q6 | B-K3 |

A piece goes after 20. ... R-KB1 21. N(6)-B5+ BxN 22. NxB+ K-B3 23. NxB discovered check!

| 21. N(4)-B5+ | BxN |
| 22. RxB! | ... |

Not 22. NxB+ K-B3 when Black barely holds since his rook still protects the knight.

22. ...	K-B1
23. NxR	RxN
24. P-N3	P-QB4

The knight has nowhere to go; 24. .... N-N3 25. R-Q7 N-R1 would be amusing.

25. R-K1

Because of the pin that the rooks exert on both the king and king-bishop files, Black loses a piece.

153. *King's Indian Defense*

Black eats a pawn, establishes his knight on the strongpoint KB5, and chokes on his ill-gotten gains.

1.	P-QB4	N-KB3
2.	N-QB3	P-KN3
3.	P-Q4	B-N2
4.	P-K4	P-Q3
5.	B-K2	0-0
6.	N-B3	P-K4
7.	P-Q5	QN-Q2

One may try to avoid Petrosjan's idea with 7. ... P-KR3 followed by N-R2 and P-B4.

8.	B-N5	P-KR3
9.	B-R4	P-KN4
10.	B-N3	N-R4
11.	P-KR4!	N-B5

White keeps a slight edge after . . . NxB 12. PxN P-N5 13. N-Q2 P-KR4 14. B-Q3 followed by N-B1-K3, tightening the grip on KB5.

12.	PxP	PxP
13.	Q-B2!	NxP+?!

Better is . . . P-KB4 14. PxP N-B4.

14.	K-Q2!	Q-B3?

Black may hold out with P-KB3, but in any case, White has more than enough for the pawn.

15.	QR-KN1	N-B5

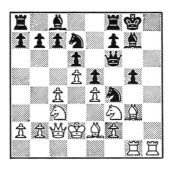

| 16. NxNP!! | B-R3 |

White wins after ... QxN 17. B-R4 Q-R3 18. B-N5 Q-N3 19. BxN!

| 17. K-K1 | N-KN3 |

If ... BxN, 18. B-R4!

18. N-K6!!	PxN
19. RxB	K-B2
20. B-R5	R-KN1
21. B-R4	

Black has insufficient resources to ward off two bishops and two rooks.

154. *King's Indian Defense*

A Noah's Ark on the king side, made possible through the courtesy of White's loose pawn on Q4.

1. P-Q4	N-KB3
2. P-QB4	P-KN3
3. N-QB3	B-N2
4. P-K4	P-Q3
5. N-B3	0-0
6. B-K2	P-K4
7. B-K3	...

A favorite of Reshevsky. The plan is to keep the tension in the center, omitting an early P-Q5 which closes the center. To counteract this idea, Black sometimes concedes to misplacing his king knight: 7. ... N-N5 8. B-N5 P-B3 9. B-R4, and eventually the knight must retreat to KR3.

7. ...	P-B3
8. 0-0	QN-Q2
9. Q-B2	...

Black has easy equality after 9. P-KR3 which consumes too much time to prevent ... N-N5, e.g., 9. P-KR3 PxP! 10. NxP R-K1 11. Q-B2 N-B4 12. P-B3, and, after ... P-Q4, White's action is stymied. 9. P-Q5 is preferable.

9. ...	N-N5!
10. B-N5	P-B3
11. B-R4?!	...

Petrosjan prefers the text, Reshevsky B-Q2.

| 11. ... | P-KR4! |

Starting the steamroller. The immediate threat is P-N4 and P-R5, ensconcing the bishop.

| 12. P-KR3 | N-R3 |
| 13. QR-Q1? | ... |

Mandatory was either PxP or P-Q5.

| 13. ... | P-KN4 |
| 14. B-N3 | P-N5! |

Driving off the queen pawn defender.

| 15. RPxP | RPxP |
| 16. N-R4 | PxP! |

Tabu is 17. RxP? P-KB4 18. RxP P-B5, and there goes a piece.

17. BxP ...

The other choice is no better: 17. N-R4 P-KB4 18. NxP NxN 19. PxN N-K4! 20. RxP! N-B6+ and still Black is better.

17. ...   **PxN**
18. P-B5   ...

White hopes for too much; the threat is 19. B-B4+ K-R1 20. P-K5 PxKP 21. N-N6+ and wins.

18. ...   **P-N4!**

Preventing the bishop check: 19. PxPe.p., NxP.

19. Q-N3+   **K-R2**
20. N-B5   **Q-K1**

It costs precious time to move the rook; besides, Black is able to win easily with two pieces for a rook.

21. NxN   **BxN**
22. BxKNP   **NxP!**
23. BxN   **BxB**
24. QxBP   **R-B2**

White gives up; a pawn for a piece is no compensation.

155. *King's Indian Defense*

The more games one sees of this opening, the more he will wonder, "Why doesn't White grab the loose pawn on Q6?"

1. P-Q4	N-KB3
2. P-QB4	P-KN3
3. N-QB3	B-N2
4. P-K4	P-Q3
5. N-B3	0-0
6. B-K2	P-K4
7. 0-0	PxP

Usually either QN-Q2 or N-B3 is played at this juncture.

8. NxP	R-K1
9. P-B3	P-B3

Hoping to pry open the center with P-Q4 and discouraging the normal deployment of White's bishop to K3.

10. N-B2	B-K3
11. N-K3?!	. . .

Better to reserve the option of returning to Q4 with this knight; 11. B-K3 is playable.

11. . . .	N-R3!
12. Q-Q2	. . .

Intending P-QN3 and B-N2. The immediate P-QN3 loses to NxKP!

12. . . .	Q-N3
13. QxP?	. . .

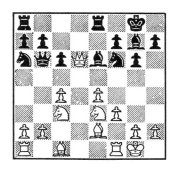

Not enough that the king knight has already moved four times; now the queen has moved twice.

13. ...	QR-Q1
14. Q-N3	N-R4
15. Q-K1	N-B5
16. K-R1	N-N5
17. P-QR3	N(N)-Q6
18. BxN	NxB
19. Q-K2	Q-N6!

Totally paralyzing the queen's wing. There's no hurry to regain the pawn.

| 20. N(B)-Q1 | R-Q2 |
| 21. R-N1 | KR-Q1 |

There isn't much to do; so White commits suicide. Longer resistance is offered by 22. P-N3.

| 22. B-Q2? | N-B5 |

Black wins material.

156. King's Indian Defense

Steinitz used to send his king on long walks around the board. When that king came home he frequently carried much booty. Here the White king does not roam but he allows himself to be the bait to lure Black into a false attack.

255

1. P-QB4	N-KB3
2. N-QB3	P-KN3
3. P-K4	P-Q3
4. P-Q4	B-N2
5. P-B3	P-K4
6. KN-K2	0-0
7. B-N5	...

Very effective since Black has already played P-K4, allowing the pin. Nevertheless, we recommend 7. . . . P-KR3.

7. ...	P-B3
8. Q-Q2	PxP
9. NxP	QN-Q2

This should have been played on move eight.

| 10. 0-0-0! | Q-N3? |

Even though less active than the text, Q-B2 is the move.

| 11. N-B2 | N-B4 |
| 12. B-K3 | B-K3? |

Because the pawn on Q6 is vulnerable, Black makes a speculative sacrifice, rather than lose the pawn outright.

| 13. P-QN4! | ... |

Often one's own king may be purposely exposed to win decisive material. Black cannot escape the pin and so hope to gain compensation in the attack.

13. ...	KR-Q1
14. B-K2	Q-B2
15. PxN	PxP
16. Q-K1	P-QN4
17. RxR+	RxR
18. PxP	PxP
19. NxP	Q-N3
20. Q-N3	R-QB1
21. R-Q1	...

We are receiving a splendid lesson in technique!

21. ...	P-QR3
22. R-Q6	Q-R4
23. N(N)-R3	P-B5
24. RxB!	PxR
25. Q-Q6	K-R1
26. QxKP	R-QN1
27. Q-Q6	R-K1
28. BxP	N-R4
29. B-N3	R-QB1
30. N-B4	Q-QN4
31. Q-Q5	Q-N1
32. N-Q6!!	

Along with White's overwhelming material superiority, Philidor's Mate is possibility: 32. ... R-B1 33. N-B7+ K-N1 34. N-R6dbl.+ K-R1 35. Q-N8+! RxQ 36. N-B7 mate.

157. *King's Indian Defense*

When you spin this one out, the spectators will hang on your every move. The opportunity to employ the queen as bait is rare indeed.

1. P-Q4	N-KB3
2. P-QB4	P-KN3
3. N-QB3	B-N2

4. P-K4	P-Q3
5. P-B3	0-0
6. B-K3	QN-Q2

The immediate 6. ... P-K4 leads to the normal lines of the Saemisch Variation in which Black plans to attack the center from another angle.

7. Q-Q2	P-B4
8. KN-K2	...

Not 8. 0-0-0 PxP! 9. BxP N-B4 with equality.

8. ...	P-QR3
9. 0-0-0	...

Menacing a pawn with PxP. The Black queen must flee the pin on the queen file!

9. ...	Q-R4
10. K-N1	...

Setting the stage for a trap into which Black is only too glad to fall.

10. ...	P-QN4?!

The last word has not been said on this variation. One point is certain, however; in practical play, Black's idea is very hard to meet.

11. N-Q5?!	...

The point: the king pawn falls with check, while the exchange of queens is accomplished—but without check. Therefore. . . .

11. ...   **NxN!**

Black's point: the queen is of no interest to him!

12. QxQ   **. . .**

White may settle for equality with 12. BPxN QxQ 13. RxQ P-B5(!), but a queen is too tempting!

| **12. ...** | **NxB** |
| **13. R-B1** | **NxBP!** |

Black has a pawn, two minor pieces and a strong initiative for the queen, but the game must be played. Good luck! Incidentally, even a grandmaster would hesitate to evaluate this position!

158. *King's Indian Defense*

A knight throws himself on the sword (10. ... N-Q5). He should have sought a more worthy cause.

1. P-Q4	N-KB3
2. P-QB4	P-KN3
3. N-QB3	B-N2
4. P-K4	P-Q3
5. P-B3	0-0
6. B-K3	N-B3
7. KN-K2	R-N1

Preparing flank action while waiting for his opponent to commit himself in the center.

8. N-B1	**P-K4**
9. N-N3	**R-K1**

The center must remain open (9. . . . PxP)!

10. P-Q5	**N-Q5?**

An attractive sacrifice, but the half-open file is inadequate compensation for the pawn.

11. NxN	**PxN**
12. BxP	**P-B4**
13. B-K3!	. . .

The refutation! After 13. PxPe.p.? PxP Black has considerable play along the queen knight and king files. The long diagonal is also a factor. Or 13. B-B2?? NxKP 14. PxN BxN+ 15. PxB RxP+ 16. K-Q2 Q-N4+ 17. K-B2 Q-B4! and White's troubles are only beginning.

13. . . .	**P-QN4**

Perhaps better is 13. . . . N-R4 and P-B4.

14. PxP	**NxKP?**

Good technique alone guarantees White the win. There is no need to hasten the end; Black tries the idea he was dreaming of—a nightmare!

15. PxN	**BxN+**
16. PxB	**RxKP**
17. Q-Q2	. . .

Not 17. Q-B3 Q-K2 18. K-Q2 B-N5 19. Q-N3 R-K1 20. R-K1 R-R5 with a winning attack.

17. ...	Q-R5+
18. P-N3	Q-K2
19. K-B2	Q-B3+
20. K-N1	B-N5
21. B-N5	Q-K4
22. B-KB4	

Black does not have enough for the pawn.

159. *King's Indian Defense*

The accepted method against the fianchetto involves shaking the defending bishop from its nest by offering a friendly exchange. White tries, but not at an acceptable moment.

1. P-Q4	N-KB3
2. P-QB4	P-KN3
3. N-KB3	B-N2
4. P-KN3	...

Both sides elect the fianchetto development of the bishop, a la Nimzovich the hypermodern.

4. ...	0-0
5. B-N2	P-B4
6. N-B3	PxP?!

This allows the queen to recapture, followed by the transfer of that dangerous piece to KR4. White will then retain his king knight for the king side attack rather than exchange this valuable piece at Q4. Unfortunately, the first player does not snatch the opportunity.

7. NxP?!	N-B3
8. 0-0	NxN
9. QxN	P-Q3
10. Q-R4	...

Other reasonable alternatives are B-N5 followed by Q-Q2, or Q-Q2 and P-N3.

| 10. ... | B-K3 |
| 11. B-N5 | ... |

Premature is 11. B-R6?! BxB! 12. QxB BxP winning a pawn.

11. ...	Q-R4
12. QR-B1	QR-B1
13. P-N3	R-B4!

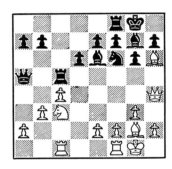

Gently coaxing White in his plan. White should consider the safe 14. B-Q2.

| 14. B-R6? | ... |

White sees he has enough for the queen after 14. ... R-R4 15. BxB RxQ 16. BxR R-R4 17. BxKP, but so does Black who has something else up his sleeve.

| 14. ... | P-KN4! |
| 15. BxNP | ... |

If the queen moves, the bishop is lost.

15. ...	RxB
16. N-Q5	R-N5
17. P-N4	QxRP
18. NxP+	K-R1
19. Q-R3	R-K1

And after 20. N-Q5 RxBP 21. P-N4 NxN, Black is up two pieces.

160. *King's Indian Defense*

Seeing the enemy plan is one thing, recognizing it as a real danger is another.

1. P-Q4	N-KB3
2. P-QB4	P-KN3
3. P-KN3	B-N2
4. B-N2	0-0
5. N-KB3	P-Q3
6. 0-0	QN-Q2
7. N-B3	P-K4
8. P-K4	P-B3
9. P-KR3	P-QR4
10. B-K3	P-R5!?

This idea of Grandmaster Lombardy has not been seriously tested in tournament play. The intention is to cramp Black's queen side and vacate a square for the queen.

11. P-Q5	PxP
12. BPxP	Q-R4
13. R-B1	N-N3!
14. Q-K2	B-Q2
15. N-Q2	KR-B1!
16. P-B4	. . .

All this follows a normal pattern. White has a trap in mind, or else he would have played P-QR3 instead of the text which undermines his own king side.

16. . . .	P-R6!

Black doesn't mind falling in!

17. P-QN4	QxNP!
18. PxP	PxP
19. R-N1	QxN
20. RxN	N-R4!

The anticipated reply was ... N-K1 when, after 21. RxQNP, Black can hardly defend his second rank.

| 21. Q-B2 | B-K1! |
| 22. RxQNP | QR-N1! |

Ruling out N-N3-B5, a maneuver intended to support P-Q6, and getting in a small sized snare of his own.

| 23. RxR | RxR |
| 24. N-N3?? | ... |

Better to postpone even a very good plan until it can be double-checked.

| 24. ... | RxN!! |

After 25. PxR P-R7 26. B-Q2 Q-N7, or 26. QxP QxB+ Black will have two pieces for a rook, enough to win the ending.

161. *King's Indian Defense*

The cluster of too many pieces on a vulnerable diagonal is a key situation that should alert a player to his opportunity.

1. P-Q4	N-KB3
2. P-QB4	P-KN3
3. P-KN3	B-N2
4. B-N2	0-0
5. N-QB3	P-Q3

6. N-B3	QN-Q2
7. 0-0	P-K4
8. P-K4	R-K1
9. P-Q5	. . .

In this variation a flexible central formation is a key concept (9. R-K1).

9. . . .	N-B4
10. Q-B2	P-QR4
11. P-N3	. . .

Preparing P-QR3, which, if played immediately, would allow the crippling 11. . . . P-R5. White aims to expel Black's knight with R-QN1 and P-QN4.

11. . . .	R-B1

Intending . . . N-K1 and P-KB4 storming the king side.

12. P-QR3	B-Q2!

White should now continue with 13. B-K3 N-K1 14. N-Q2, after which he is poised for P-QN4.

13. R-N1??	. . .

White's method had to include N-Q2, for Black always has the defense . . . P-R5 14. P-QN4 N-N6! But now Black also has something else!

13. . . .	N(4)xKP!!
14. NxN	NxN

That's the game. White has lost a vital central pawn: 15. QxN B-B4 winning the rook; 15. NxKP N-B4 16. N-Q3 B-B4! merely winning.

162. *King's Indian Defense*

An exposed queen and a king on an open file is the clue to a winning combination. One learns to create the situation.

1. P-Q4	N-KB3
2. P-QB4	P-KN3
3. N-QB3	B-N2
4. P-K4	P-Q3
5. N-B3	0-0
6. P-KN3	P-K4
7. B-N2	N-B3

Afraid unduly of the following line: 8. 0-0 PxP 9. NxP NxP 10. N(4)xN NxN 11. NxQ NxQ 12. NxNP BxN! 13. BxB QR-N1 14. RxN RxB 15. R-N1 R-K1 with chances for both sides, White consents to. . . .

8. P-Q5?!	N-Q5!

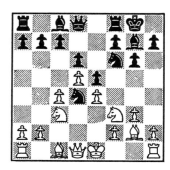

Now best is 9. B-K3, forcing the exchange of knights.

9. NxN?!	PxN

Still possible is 10. N-K2 R-K1 11. P-B3 P-B4 12. PxPe.p. PxP 13. NxP Q-N3 and all we can say is that Black has ample play for the pawn. But a pawn is a pawn!

| **10. QxP??** | **NxKP!!** |

If 11. QxN, R-K1 wins the queen; or 11. Q-Q3 NxN 12. PxN B-B4 13. Q-Q2 R-K1+ and total collapse is only a matter of time.

163. *King's Indian Defense*

The theory on this line was established in 1954 in the game Denker versus Bronstein, USA-USSR Match, New York City. At that time commentators affixed the derogatory mark to 8. Q-B2(?), which judgment proved correct, as the game went: 8. ... PxP! 9. NxP N-N3 10. P-N3?! P-B4! 11. KN-N5 P-QR3 12. N-R3 B-B4 13. Q-Q2 P-Q4 and Bronstein's skill prevailed. Until two years ago, nobody had questioned the validity of Bronstein's *trap.* But more recently White had his finest hour, for he meets a rival well acquainted with the old line, but not at all with the new nuances!

1. P-Q4	N-KB3
2. P-QB4	P-KN3
3. N-QB3	B-N2
4. P-KN3	O-O
5. B-N2	P-Q3
6. N-B3	QN-Q2
7. O-O	P-K4
8. Q-B2!!	

The extra credit is for perseverence; the move is reinstated!

8. ...	PxP
9. NxP	N-N3
10. R-Q1	. . .

Of course! The very idea of the opening is to apply immediate pressure along the queen file. 10. Q-Q3 is also a good idea, but untried in tournament play.

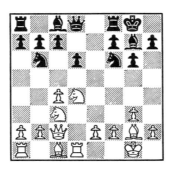

| 10. . . . | NxP |

Naturally if 10. . . . P-B4, 11. N(4)-N5 and the queen pawn is lost.

| 11. QN-N5! | P-QR3 |

Obviously the black knight cannot retreat because of NxBP.

| 12. QxN | PxN |
| 13. NxP | B-Q2?! |

Lombardy-Saidy, US Championship 1968 continued 13. . . . N-K1 (slightly better than the above text.) 14. Q-B2 Q-K2 15. B-B4 B-B4 16. P-K4 B-Q2 17. N-B3 N-B3 and, although White has a slight edge, a draw resulted.

14. B-N5!	P-R3
15. B-B4	P-N4
16. B-K3	N-N5
17. B-Q4	N-K4
18. BxN	BxB
19. BxP!	R-N1
20. B-B6	BxB
21. QxB	R-N3
22. Q-B4	Q-N1
23. P-QR4	P-B3
24. N-R3	P-Q4
25. Q-B5	B-Q3
26. Q-B2	RxP
27. QxBP	. . .

White is winning by attrition. With a pawn plus he's perfectly willing to trade blows.

27. . . .	RxP
28. N-N5	B-K4
29. QR-B1	Q-R1
30. QxRP	QxP
31. QxP+	B-N2
32. N-Q4	

Black resigns, for 35. N-B5 cannot be prevented.

164. *King's Indian Defense*

At precisely the right moment White doubles his opponent's pawns and then goes to work on them.

1. P-Q4	N-KB3
2. P-QB4	P-KN3
3. P-KN3	B-N2
4. B-N2	0-0
5. N-KB3	P-Q3
6. 0-0	P-B4
7. PxP	PxP
8. N-K5?!	. . .

White moves a piece twice in the opening, but he does have method. Creating the illusion of gaining easy equality, he affords Black the opportunity to exchange queens, eliminating the danger of such heavyweights in a precarious situation.

8. . . .	KN-Q2?!

After 8. . . . QN-Q2 9. N-Q3, Black is cramped. Perhaps best is 8. . . . Q-B2, for if 9. B-B4, then P-KN4 wins a piece.

9. N-Q3!	. . .

Avoiding premature, simplifying exchanges.

9. ...	N-K4?!
10. NxN!	BxN
11. N-B3	N-B3

Black does not double White's pawns (11. ... BxN) because, unable to force an immediate ending, he would be subject to attack. Unfortunately, possessed of excessive faith in the power of the bishops versus knights, he walks right into the loss.

12. B-R6!	...

First, development with tempo gain.

12. ...	R-K1
13. BxN!!	...

Since his rook hangs, Black cannot reciprocate with 13. ... BxN, so that only he will have to bear the burden of shattered pawns.

13. ...	PxB
14. QxQ	...

Second, simplification to an ending.

14. ...	RxQ
15. N-R4	B-B4
16. QR-B1	B-Q5
17. P-N3	

Finally, Black's resignation, since his weak queen side pawns cannot long be defended.

165. *King's Indian Defense*

Two bishops are a force to be reckoned with, but not without exception!

1. P-Q4	P-KN3
2. P-QB4	B-N2
3. N-QB3	P-Q3
4. P-K4	P-K4

The game Botvinnik (the then World's Champion) vs. Lombardy (the then World's Junior Champion), Munich, 1958, continued 5. PxP PxP 6. QxQ+ KxQ 7. B-N5+ P-B3 8. 0-0-0+ N-Q2 9. B-K3 P-B3 10. P-KN3 K-B2 11. P-B4 N-R3! 12. P-KR3 N-B2 13. N-B3 B-R3! 14. R-K1 R-K1 with an excellent game for Black. The point is that White must exercise extreme caution in considering 5. PxP with the subsequent queen swap.

5. B-K3?	. . .

An incautious move violating the rule of developing knights before bishops, KN-K2 or N-KB3 and then B-K3.

5. . . .	PxP!
6. BxP	N-KB3

Black intends to gain time attacking the queen bishop with N-QB3; he therefore avoids an even exchange. In any case, his own bishop is necessary to the defense of the king.

7. B-K2	0-0
8. N-B3	B-N5
9. 0-0	R-K1

Calmly mounting pressure against the center.

10. P-KR3	BxN

Black rightly rids himself of one bishop for a precious knight which so ably defended the dark squares. White's normally potent king bishop is left without scope, corralled by his own pawns.

11. BxB	N-B3
12. B-K3	N-Q2
13. Q-Q2	N-B4
14. QR-K1	P-QR4

Stable-izing the knight on QB4.

| 15. B-N5? | . . . |

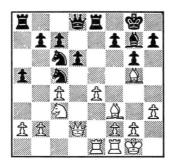

At last, another opportunity to shed the other bishop. The game is even after 15. B-B4.

| 15. . . . | BxN!! |

Compelling White to accept doubled pawns, which are not only ready targets for the knights but also totally impede the action of the legendary two bishops.

16. PxB	P-B3
17. B-R4	N-K4
18. B-Q1	P-KN4
19. B-KN3	K-R1
20. B-B2	R-N1
21. P-B4	PxP
22. BxP	Q-Q2
23. BxN	BPxN

With his pawns in a shambles, White has a lost position, but correct technique must be applied to win!

166. *King's Indian Defense*

There never was a game so short but so extraordinary in combinational content. Arthur Feuerstein, an exceptionally talented master gives us this gem.

1. P-Q4	N-KB3
2. P-QB4	P-B3
3. P-Q5	. . .

The text prevents a reversion to a Slav Defense.

3. . . .	PxP

Better is . . . P-Q3 maintaining the tension.

4. PxP	P-KN3
5. N-QB3	Q-R4?!

Black is getting the idea and so White leads him on with the next move.

6. P-KN3!	N-K5?

Black ought to admit the error of his ways and simply play . . . B-N2, P-Q3 and 0-0.

7. Q-Q4!	NxN
8. B-Q2!	QxQP??

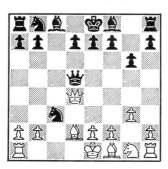

Both queens eye a cornered rook, but White has has another potent point. Black should have humbly defended with 8. . . . P-B3, closing the deadly diagonal.

9. QxN!!   . . .

The dual threats of QxB mate and QxR cannot both be parried.

    9. . . .   **N-B3**

Fair exchange is no robbery, but there's more!

10. QxR!	**N-Q5**
11. R-B1!	**QxR**
12. QxN!	**QxN**

So far nobody's hurt.

    13. QxRP!!

Black's other rook also goes, for if 13. . . . RxQ, then 14. RxB mate!

167. *King's Indian Reversed*

Excessive zeal for the attack plus inordinate greed for a sickly king pawn hastens defeat.

1. N-KB3	N-KB3
2. P-KN3	P-QN4
3. B-N2	B-N2
4. 0-0	P-K3
5. P-Q3	P-Q4
6. QN-Q2	P-B4
7. P-K4	B-K2
8. P-K5	. . .

The same theme is found in the French Defense, the strong-point K5 as the focal point for the attack.

8. . . .	KN-Q2
9. R-K1	N-QB3
10. N-B1	P-N4?

The natural reaction is to devise a method of undermining that strong-point. The text, however, only weakens the Black king side. A sharper plan is 10. . . . Q-N3 and 0-0-0.

| 11. P-KR3 | P-KR4 |
| 12. P-B3 | P-KN5 |

Willy-nilly, Black intends to bowl over his opponent and must take the consequences.

13. PxP	PxP
14. N(3)-R2	N(3)xP
15. P-Q4	N-B6+

Since Black cannot hold the knight pawn, he tries to surrender it under favorable circumstances. But the damage is done.

| 16. NxN | PxN |
| 17. QxP | PxP |

Black should not open the queen bishop file!

18. PxP	N-B3
19. B-B4	N-K5
20. QR-B1	B-Q3
21. N-Q2	Q-N1
22. BxB	. . .

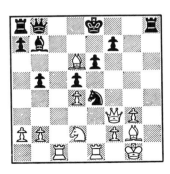

If . . . NxN(?), 23. Q-B6 wins the exchange.

22. . . .	QxB
23. N-N3	R-Q1
24. N-B5	. . .

White prefers to swap knights on his own terms.

24. . . .	B-R1
25. R-B2	K-B1
26. R(1)-QB1	R-R3
27. N-Q3!	

Reasonable technique will net the point. Black has a useless bishop while White has absolute control of the queen bishop file, a vehicle for decisive penetration of the enemy camp. The Black forces are totally uncoordinated.

168. *King's Indian Reversed*

The Black pawns resemble the crumbling columns of an ancient ruin. Double pawns are bad enough, but double and triple pawns must constitute a lost position. After White wangled a won game, undoubtedly his inexperience prevented him from capitalizing on the edge. The columns came crashing down, trapping the novice in the rubble.

1. N-KB3	P-Q4
2. P-KN3	P-QB3
3. B-N2	B-N5
4. P-Q3	BxN?!

The text wastes a tempo, gives up a bishop for a knight without cause, and allows White a powerful grip on the center with his advanced, double king bishop pawn. Better is 4. . . . N-Q2.

5. PxB!	N-B3
6. 0-0	P-K3
7. N-Q2	B-K2

| 8. P-KB4 | 0-0 |
| 9. N-B3 | P-B4?! |

Losing more time and weakening the long White diagonal; 9. . . . P-QR4 in conjunction with Q-N3 is a better plan.

| 10. N-K5 | N-B3?! |

10. . . . N-Q2 also develops the knight, without harming the pawn structure.

11. NxN	PxN
12. P-B4!	R-N1
13. R-K1	R-K1
14. Q-R4?!	. . .

The queen plays right field better. More to the point is 14. P-N3 without delay.

| 14. . . . | B-B1 |
| 15. P-N3 | . . . |

Not 15. QxBP PxP 16. PxP Q-Q5 with good play for Black.

15. . . .	Q-B1
16. B-N2	R-Q1
17. P-B5	. . .

White has a light-squared bishop; so naturally he works on the light squares.

17. . . .	KPxP
18. BxN!	PxB
19. B-R3!	PxP

Black opens the position in an attempt to obtain play.

| 20. QPxP | R-Q7 |
| 21. R-K3 | Q-Q2 |

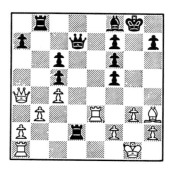

Obviously White is slightly better, but he cannot afford to be careless.

    22. K-N2??   . . .

A meaningless waiting move that loses instantly. White could have continued to apply the pressure with 22. R-KB3(!).

22. . . .	Q-Q5!
23. R(1)-K1	R-K1!!

If White nabs the rook, he gets mated.

24. K-N1	P-B5!
25. PxP	QxKBP
26. R-N3+	K-R1
27. R-KB1	R-K8!!

Checkmate is inevitable.

169. *King's Indian Reversed*

A knight developed on a weak square versus one firmly lodged on the strong central point Q5.

1. N-KB3	P-KN3
2. P-KN3	B-N2
3. B-N2	P-Q3
4. P-Q3	P-K4
5. P-K4	N-QB3

6. N-B3	KN-K2
7. B-K3	0-0
8. Q-Q2	N-Q5!

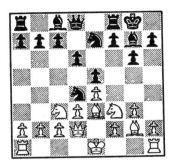

Preventing the freeing maneuver P-Q4. White is tempted immediately to oust the intruding knight, and it is precisely this impatience that leads him to a violent end.

| 9. N-K2?? | B-R6!! |

The bishop is immune because of NxN+ winning the queen. 10. 0-0 loses the exchange: NxN(6)+ 11. BxN BxR; or 10. K-B1 NxN(6) and a piece goes; finally, 10. R-KN1 loses a piece to BxB!

10. N(3)xN	BxB!
11. R-KN1	PxN
12. NxP	P-QB4
13. N-N5	B-B6
14. P-KN4	. . .

This desperate attempt to trap the queen bishop allows Black to present the reader with a superb mating attack.

14. . . .	P-Q4!
15. BxP	R-B1
16. B-R3	PxP
17. PxP	Q-N3!
18. BxN	QxN
19. BxR	QxP

| 20. BxB | KxB |
| 21. R-QB1 | R-Q1! |

If 22. QxR, QxR+ and mate next.

22. Q-K3	QxBP
23. R-N3	Q-Q8+
24. RxQ	RxR

Checkmate!

170. *King's Indian Reversed*

Black tries a Caro-Kann (1. ... P-QB3), but White prefers
a King's Indian Reversed (2. P-Q3). The trappy theme ex-
emplified here is seen in many king-pawn openings. Either
central pawn, depending on the situation, is shoved down,
even sacrificed if necessary, to block the enemy development.
Time is the crucial element—and again, the pin!

1. P-K4	P-QB3
2. P-Q3	P-Q4
3. N-Q2	PxP
4. PxP	N-B3
5. KN-B3	B-N5
6. P-KR3	B-R4?

The pin doesn't hold; so Black should give his bishop for
the knight. Now comes the king pawn, for the bishop no
longer defends his own K3.

| 7. P-K5 | N-Q4 |
| 8. P-K6! | P-B3 |

Much better is 8. ... N-B2.

9. P-KN4	B-N3
10. N-Q4	N-B2
11. P-QB3	Q-Q4
12. Q-N3!	...

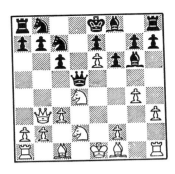

Black is paralyzed; so that his best chance to reduce the virulence of White's attack lay in the swap of the queens. But temptation is too great.

| 12. ... | QxR? |
| 13. QxP | K-Q1 |

The only way to defend mate without enormous material loss.

| 14. N(2)-B3! | B-Q6 |
| 15. B-B4!! | ... |

Where mate is concerned, spare no horses—or bishops for that matter.

15. ...	QxB+
16. K-Q2	QxP+
17. KxB	NxP

The point is that after 17. ... N(1)-R3 18. K-B4 and White's rook decisively enters the fray.

18. NxN+	K-K1
19. Q-B8+	K-B2
20. N(3)-N5+	PxN
21. NxP+	K-B3
22. Q-K6	

Black is checkmated.

171. *Nimzo–Indian Defense*

The tension trap: the longer it is there the more attractive appears the bait. Perhaps the tasty morsel can be snatched from its perch without touching off the spring which by now must be rusty. Perhaps no one is looking. Perhaps!

1. P-Q4	N-KB3
2. P-QB4	P-K3
3. N-QB3	B-N5
4. N-B3	P-Q4
5. PxP	PxP
6. B-N5	P-KR3
7. B-R4	P-B4
8. P-K3	0-0
9. PxP	QN-Q2
10. B-K2	Q-R4

Right from the start Black is overanxious to pursue White's seemingly weak pawns. To be considered is 10. ... NxP 11. 0-0 BxN 12. PxB B-K3.

11. 0-0	BxN
12. PxB	QxP(4)

Should Black capture the other bishop pawn, White would have a ready-made bind on the queen knight pawn, which would be restrained by the advanced bishop pawn.

13. R-B1	P-QN3
14. P-B4	B-N2
15. N-Q4	QR-B1?

Whatever this move is supposed to accomplish, this goal is surely overshadowed by the danger to the queen on the open file.

16. B-B3!!	Q-N5

Now Black cannot conveniently escape this deadly pin.

17. P-QR3!	QxRP?

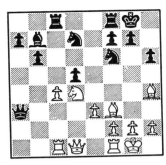

Allowing the queen further to be buffeted about is much the better choice, e.g., 17. ... Q-R4 18. N-N3 Q-R5 19. PxP RxR 20. NxR QxP with good counterchances.

18. R-R1	Q-B4
19. RxP	B-R1
20. Q-R1!	...

Tightening the bind by preventing 20. ... PxP.

| 20. ... | K-R2 |
| 21. R-Q1 | QxP |

Losing patience, Black finally takes the bait. Correct is 21. ... KR-K1, although, as a result of his unimaginative play, Black is already in a bad way.

| 22. B-K2!! | Q-B6 |

Eventually Black must submit to the ax waiting for him at QB6.

23. RxB!

After 23. ... QxQ, 24. R(8)xQ keeps the piece.

172. Nimzo–Indian Defense

Attack, counter-attack—nothing of the sort. But one careless move and Black lowers the boom.

1. P-Q4	N-KB3
2. P-QB4	P-K3
3. N-QB3	B-N5
4. P-K3	0-0
5. B-Q3	P-Q4
6. N-B3	P-QN3

Tartakover's Defense is being resurrected these days.

7. 0-0	B-N2
8. PxP	PxP
9. N-K5	. . .

Less active but more precise is Q-K2 and R-Q1. White then applies pressure on Black's queen pawn by playing B-R6, at the right moment, knocking out the fianchettoed defender.

9. . . .	B-Q3
10. N-N5	B-K2
11. Q-B2	. . .

A "grandmaster draw" is had after 11. N-QB3 B-Q3 12. N-N5 etc.

11. . . .	P-B4
12. P-QN3	P-QR3!
13. N-QB3	N-B3
14. NxN?!	. . .

More consistent is R-Q1.

14. . . .	BxN
15. N-K2	B-N2

Now Black has equality, but he wants more.

16. B-N2	P-N3!

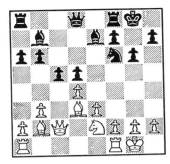

A fine waiting move. The natural move has been long in coming, but here it comes—at the wrong time!

17. QR-Q1?	P-B5!!
18. PxP	PxP
19. QxP	. . .

After 19. BxBP R-B1 20. Q-N3 P-QN4 21. B-Q3 B-Q4, White loses the queen.

| 19. ... | R-B1 |
| 20. Q-N3 | B-Q4! |

Fate waits for the queen: 21. Q-R4 P-QN4 22. QxRP R-R1 23. QxP R-R4!

173. *Nimzo–Indian Defense*

The queen threatens mate and forces a pawn weakening in the enemy camp. She should then return to base; she doesn't!

1. P-Q4	N-KB3
2. P-QB4	P-K3
3. N-QB3	B-N5
4. P-K3	0-0
5. B-Q3	P-Q4
6. N-B3	P-QN3
7. 0-0	B-N2
8. P-QR3	B-Q3

The retreat to K2 is smoother.

9. P-QN4	PxP
10. BxP	QN-Q2
11. B-N2	P-QR4

No better is 11. . . . P-B4 12. QPxP! PxP 13. P-N5! when the active queen side majority forces Black to the defensive.

12. PxP!	RxP
13. N-QN5	B-K2
14. P-QR4	N-K5
15. B-Q3	N-Q3

There's no reason to retreat; 15. . . . N(Q)-B3 is correct.

16. Q-K2	N-B3
17. KR-B1	NxN?

The better deployment of White's king bishop is certainly not fostered by 17. . . . P-B3!

18. BxN	P-B4
19. N-K5!	Q-Q4!
20. P-B3	PxP?

Encouraging White's advance. The queen should have retreated, but Black is unaware of the danger.

21. BxP!	B-B4
22. BxB	PxB
23. Q-N2	

Because the queen may be trapped in the center, the queen bishop pawn is lost. If 23. .... R-Q1, 24. B-B4! Q-Q3 25. NxBP KxN 26. QxB+ etc.

174. *Nimzo–Indian Defense*

There are times when *luft* (fresh air for the king who must escape a check by a rook or queen on the first rank) is imperative.

1. P-Q4	N-KB3
2. P-QB4	P-K3
3. N-QB3	B-N5
4. P-K3	0-0
5. B-Q3	P-Q4
6. N-B3	P-QN3
7. P-QR3	B-K2
8. PxP	PxP
9. P-QN4	P-B4
10. QPxP	PxP
11. PxP	BxP
12. 0-0	Q-K2
13. B-N2	N-B3
14. Q-R4	B-N2
15. KR-B1	B-Q3
16. Q-R4	. . .

Both sides have completed their development. Even though he is saddled with an isolated pawn, Black has sufficient counterplay. Unfortunately, he is overconfident that he has more.

| 16. ... | N-K4?? |
| 17. NxN!! | ... |

If 17. ... QxN, 18. N-R4 P-Q5 (18. ... Q-KR4 19. BxN!) 19. BxP Q-Q4 20. P-B3 and wins. Or 17. ... BxN 18. BxP+, winning a pawn.

175. *Nimzo–Indian Defense*

Black does indeed fall into the opening trap but the game is not over yet! Given time to regroup, his counter-stroke socks his rival right off his rocker.

1. P-Q4	N-KB3
2. P-QB4	P-K3
3. N-QB3	B-N5
4. P-K3	0-0
5. N-B3	P-B4
6. B-Q3	P-Q4
7. 0-0	QN-Q2
8. P-QR3	B-R4

Fifteen years ago BxN was all the rage.

| 9. B-Q2 | P-QR3 |
| 10. N-K5! | B-N3! |

Black does not exchange knights allowing White to build a pawn mass in the center. By applying pressure on the queen pawn he hopes to cajole White into doing the exchanging.

| 11. BPxP | BPxP |
| 12. KPxP | BxP? |

Either NxP or PxP was adequate.

| 13. NxP!! | RxN |
| 14. PxP | . . . |

With fork in hand the pawn may spear his supper.

14. . . .	R-B1
15. PxN	BxP
16. N-K2?!	. . .

After N-K4 White should easily realize his pawn plus.

16. . . .	B-R2
17. P-R3	B-B3
18. B-B4+	K-R1
19. N-N3??	. . .

There were so many better moves that White's losing text is impossible to explain. He could safely have played: B-B3, QB-N5, B-N4 or even the apparently awkward B-K3.

| 19. . . . | Q-B2 |
| 20. Q-N3 | N-N5!! |

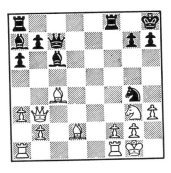

How easy it is to lose a won game!

| 21. PxN | R-B6!! |

If 22. PxR, then QxN+ 23. K-R1 BxP+ etc.; or if 22. Q-B2, then simply RxN and White cannot avoid mate.

| 22. N-B5 | RxQ |
| 23. BxR | Q-N3 |

After the QN pawn falls White's game collapses.

176. Nimzo–Indian Defense

Time after time White flits about with the queen. Yet Black makes but one queen sally and he inherits total collapse!

1. P-Q4	N-KB3
2. P-QB4	P-K3
3. N-QB3	B-N5
4. P-K3	0-0
5. B-Q3	P-Q4
6. N-B3	P-B4
7. 0-0	QPxP
8. BxP	QN-Q2
9. Q-K2!	. . .

Preparing the advance P-K4 and the natural centralization of the rooks at K1 and Q1.

9. . . .	P-QR3
10. P-QR3	. . .

If Black wants *lebensraum* on the queen side, White should thwart that plan with P-QR4.

10. . . .	PxP
11. PxP	B-K2

Losing time. But how was the hapless prelate to know that he would be vulnerable on the king file? Better was 11. . . . BxN.

12. R-K1	N-N3
13. B-Q3	B-Q2
14. N-K5	N(N)-Q4
15. Q-B3	B-B3
16. Q-R3!	Q-N3?

But White's last didn't even look like a threat!

17. NxN!	BxN
18. N-Q7	

Black could have played 17. PxN when there would follow 18. NxB and RxB!

177. *Nimzo–Indian Defense*

A similar trap occurs after 1. P-Q4 P-Q4 2. P-QB4 P-K3 3. PxP PxP 4. N-QB3 N-KB3 5. B-N5 P-B3 6. Q-B2 P-KR3? 7. BxN, QxB 8. NxP and if PxN, then 9. QxB+ wins.

1. P-Q4	N-KB3
2. P-QB4	P-K3
3. N-QB3	B-N5
4. P-K3	P-B4
5. N-K2	N-K5
6. Q-B2	PxP
7. PxP	P-Q4
8. P-QR3	NxN
9. NxN	B-K2?

Correct is 9. . . . . BxN+.

10. PxP	PxP
11. NxP!!	. . .

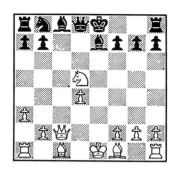

Observe: 11. . . . QxN 12. QxB+!

| 11. . . . | N-B3 |
| 12. NxB | NxP |

The pawn must be recaptured.

13. Q-B3	QxN+
14. B-K3	N-B4
15. B-N5+	B-Q2
16. BxB+	QxB
17. B-B5!	N-K2

Else Black cannot castle. After 17. ... Q-K3+ 18. K-B1, White's impending R-K1 wins easily.

| 18. 0-0 | 0-0 |
| 19. QR-Q1 | N-Q4 |

After 19. ... Q-B2, 20. KR-K1 wins at least the exchange.

| 20. BxR | RxB |
| 21. Q-B3 | |

An exchange is enough to win here.

178. *Orangutan Opening*

This opening, named after a gangling ape, was so dubbed at a time when 1. P-K4 and 1. P-Q4 were thought to be the only normal and therefore the only satisfactory debuts. Today such grandmasters as Pal Benko, Bent Larsen and William Lombardy have brought the opening into true prominence so that 1. P-QN4 may be considered as regular as any other opening. The obvious theme is the early attempt to gain a central pawn for a flank pawn, an exceptionally good bargain.

| 1. P-QN4 | P-K4 |
| 2. B-N2 | BxP? |

Better bolster the center with . . . P-KB3.

3. BxP	N-KB3
4. N-KB3	P-Q4
5. P-K3	B-Q3
6. B-N2	. . .

The queen bishop, with its sweep of the long diagonal, is too valuable to exchange.

6. . . .	P-B4
7. B-K2	0-0
8. 0-0	B-B4
9. P-B4	N-B3
10. PxP	NxP
11. N-B3	N(4)-N5?!

Time is of the essence; therefore, 11. . . . NxN instead.

| 12. P-Q4! | PxP |
| 13. PxP | N-B7? |

Not every fork wins; ... N-K2 controls the Q4 square.

| 14. P-Q5! | NxR |

If ... N(3)-N5, 15. R-B1 will win two pieces for a rook after 16. P-QR3.

15. PxN!	N-B7
16. PxP	R-N1
17. Q-Q5!	...

The attack on the queen bishop gains the needed time to defend the forward pawn and introduce the king rook into play.

| 17. ... | B-N3 |
| 18. R-Q1 | B-R6 |

Or 18. ... B-K2 19. Q-K5! Q-K1 20. N-Q5 and it's mate or a piece.

19. QxQ	KRxQ
20. RxR+	RxR
21. BxB	NxB
22. N-K5!!	

Black must lose his rook for the queen knight pawn.

179. Queen's Indian Defense

White assumes a weakness for the dubious prospect of future attack.

1. P-Q4	N-KB3
2. P-QB4	P-K3
3. N-KB3	P-QN3
4. P-KN3	B-N2
5. B-N2	B-K2
6. 0-0	0-0
7. N-B3	N-K5

Either the text or ... P-Q4 effectively prevents P-K4.

8. Q-B2	NxN
9. PxN?	. . .

Absolutely better is 9. QxN.

9. . . .	N-B3
10. N-K5	N-R4
11. BxB	NxB
12. P-B5!	P-Q3!

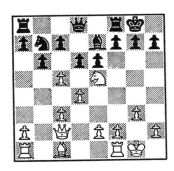

In this case dissolving one weakness creates another just as glaring—a backward pawn on an open file.

13. N-B6	Q-Q2
14. NxB+	QxN
15. Q-K4	N-R4
16. PxQP	PxP
17. B-B4	QR-B1
18. QR-B1	R-B5

White is positionally busted.

180. Queen's Indian Defense (By Transposition)

A premature fianchetto results in a misguided bishop.

1. P-KN3	P-Q4
2. B-N2	N-KB3
3. N-KB3	P-QN3?

Normally . . . P-B4 and N-B3 provide active play.

4. P-B4!   **P-K3?!**

Better is . . . P-B3.

5. PxP!   **PxP?!**

Now . . . NxP will keep the lines open for the bishop.

6. 0-0   **B-Q3**
7. P-Q4   **0-0?!**

Premature; 7. . . . QN-Q2 guards against N-K5.

8. N-B3   **P-B3?!**

If the intention is still . . . B-N2, then the text readies the bishop for burial. Correct is . . . QN-Q2 9. N-QN5 B-K2 10. N-K5 B-N2 11. B-B4 P-B3 with equality.

9. N-K5!   **B-N2**

. . . P-KR3 would prevent B-N5, a move needed to enforce the P-K4 break.

10. B-N5   **P-KR3**
11. BxN   **QxB**
12. P-B4!   . . .

Permanently anchoring the knight.

12. . . .   **R-Q1?**

Better is . . . Q-K2, preparing . . . N-Q2 and retaining the possibility of . . . P-B3, ousting the knight.

13. P-K4   **PxP**
14. NxKP   **Q-K2**
15. Q-N3!   **N-R3**

Not . . . N-Q2 16. QR-B1 QR-B1 17. B-R3! And if . . . P-B4, 16. NxKBP! QxN 17. QxQ+ and wins. Finally, 15. . . . BxN 16. BPxN! RxP 17. N-Q6!

16. QR-B1   **QR-B1**
17. B-R3!   . . .

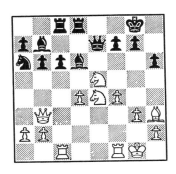

The recurring theme of the weak king bishop pawn.

17. ...	**P-B4**

After ... R-B2 18. NxKBP QxN(2)? 19. B-K6!

18. **BxR**	**BxB**
19. **NxB**	**RxN**
20. **PxP**	**NxP**
21. **QxP+**	**QxQ**
22. **NxQ**	**R-Q7**

If ... KxN, 23. P-QN4.

23. **N-K5**	**...**

Not 23. P-QN4 B-R6!

23. ...	**RxNP**
24. **R-KB2**	**RxR**
25. **KxR**	**B-K3**
26. **P-QR3**	

And White wins by attrition.

181. *Queen's Fianchetto (Larsen's) Opening*

Aware of his opponent's penchant for the bizarre, Black bides his time, patiently building his position with purely natural developing moves. When the opening begins to stall from an overdosage of listless play, White panics, desperately tries to close the position and, as a result, seals in his own king.

1. P-QN3	P-K4
2. B-N2	N-QB3
3. P-QB4	N-B3
4. N-KB3?!	. . .

Overconfidence in an opening system without thought to a proper plan. Better to proceed with N-QB3, P-N3, B-N2 and then P-Q3, or even N-KB3 (or N-KR3).

4. . . .	P-K5!
5. N-Q4	B-B4
6. NxN	QPxN

One logical developing move follows another. Black does not hesitate to accept doubled pawns as he has the open queen file and the better development to more than compensate for that factor.

7. P-K3	B-B4
8. B-K2	Q-K2
9. Q-B2	0-0-0

Now White should continue with either N-B3 and 0-0-0, or P-QR3, intending immediate queen side expansion. Instead he wrongly attempts to close the king side. If he feared N-KN5

(or N-Q2)-K4, he should have played P-KR3; then he is ready to meet N-Q2 with P-B4.

10. P-B4?	N-N5!
11. P-N3	. . .

Because of Q-R5+, White cannot drive out the knight with P-KR3.

11. . . .	P-KR4!!
12. P-KR3??	. . .

Still unplayable. White's last hope remained in P-KR4, blocking the king side pawns. Then, of course, the Black knight would remain a thorn in his side, but that surely does not spell checkmate.

12. . . .	P-R5!
13. PxN	. . .

There is little choice as RPxP was threatened. Naturally, White cannot play 13. PxP himself, allowing QxP+!

13. . . .	PxP!
14. R-N1	. . .

After 14. RxR RxR 15. PxB R-R8+ 16. B-B1 P-N7, Black promotes to a new queen.

14. . . .	R-R8!!

A startling sacrifice achieving a speedy conclusion. This is what White overlooked, and so, no doubt, would anyone else. 15. RxR P-N7 16. R-N1 Q-R5+ 17. K-Q1 Q-R7 18. RxP Q-R8+ 19. B-B1 QxB mate!

15. RxR	P-N7
16. R-B1	Q-R5+
17. K-Q1	PxR=Q+

White's had it. After 18. BxQ Q-R8 19. K-K1 BxNP, or 18. . . . Q-B7 19. B-R3 Q-N8+ 20. K-K2 Q-R7+ 21. K-K1 Q-N6+ 22. K-Q1 QxB, the king still does not escape.

182. *Queen's Gambit*

Poor planning, panic, desultory opening play, each one alone is good reason for a loss.

1.	P-Q4	N-KB3
2.	P-QB4	P-K3
3.	N-QB3	P-Q4
4.	B-N5	B-K2
5.	P-K3	0-0
6.	R-B1	P-KR3
7.	B-R4	P-B3
8.	N-B3	QN-Q2
9.	B-Q3	PxP
10.	BxP	P-QN4
11.	B-Q3	B-N2
12.	0-0	P-R3
13.	P-R4	. . .

Impeding the freeing maneuver . . . P-B4.

13.	. . .	PxP
14.	NxP	Q-R4
15.	N-Q2	QR-B1
16.	N-K4!	. . .

The pin pushes Black's panic button after which the king side is weakened. He should play 16. . . . Q-Q1.

16. . . .	P-N4?
17. NxN+	NxN
18. N-B5!	PxB

After 18. . . . BxN 19. RxB Q-N5 20. BxP PxB 21. RxP+ K-R1 22. Q-B3 forces mate, while 18. . . . B-R1 is self-entombment.

19. NxB	Q-KN4
20. Q-B3	R-B2
21. BxP	Q-Q4
22. Q-B4	

White wins at least one more pawn.
What else?

183. *Queen's Gambit*

General rule: In the Tartakover Defense the queen bishop usually functions more effectively on K3.

1. P-Q4	N-KB3
2. P-QB4	P-K3
3. N-KB3	P-Q4
4. N-B3	B-K2
5. B-N5	0-0
6. P-K3	P-QN3

The trademark of the Tartakover Defense, one idea of which is acceptance of central hanging pawns, usually a debility, in return for an aggressive posture, the bishop pair and a generally fluid game. Hanging pawns are those which stand freely without the support of a pawn base or pawn chain. "Hanging Pawns" lend a position attacking possibilities for their proud owner, but they may be a grave debility in an ending, or even in a middle game in which the attack has faltered.

7. BxN?!	. . .

This capture should be delayed (B-R4) until Black has committed his queen bishop.

| 7. . . . | BxB |
| 8. B-Q3 | B-N2? |

Correct is P-B4, and if 9. QPxP, then NPxP 10. PxP BxN+ 11. PxB PxP with easy equality. Black's bishop then goes to K3 and his knight to B3.

| 9. PxP | PxP |
| 10. P-KR4! | . . . |

Marshall's idea with which Black is totally unfamiliar, for he falls right in line with disaster.

| 10. . . . | R-K1 |
| 11. Q-B2 | P-N3? |

Providing the necessary target. Black must defend this threat: 11. BxP+ KxB 12. N-N5+ BxN 13. PxB+ K-N1 14. Q-R5 with menacing prospects. Black should try: 11. . . . P-KR3 12. P-KN4 P-B4 13. P-N5 BPxP! 14. PxB QxP and he is actually on the attack.

| 12. P-R5 | N-Q2? |

Perhaps . . . K-N2!

| 13. PxP | RPxP |

All exits are now shut tight.

14. BxP!	PxB

What else?

15. QxP+	B-N2
16. N-KN5	Q-K2
17. R-R8+!!	KxR
18. Q-R7	Checkmate!

184. *Queen's Gambit*

The pieces that rely on an *overloaded piece* are sitting ducks. White waits in the bushes. Black simply develops and loses simply.

1. P-Q4	N-KB3
2. P-QB4	P-K3
3. N-KB3	P-B4
4. P-K3	P-Q4
5. N-B3	BPxP
6. KPxP	B-K2
7. PxP	NxP

An even game results after 7. ... PxP, but Black decides to take his chances by continuing the attack against the isolated pawn.

8. B-Q3	N-QB3
9. 0-0	0-0
10. R-K1	N(3)-N5
11. B-N1	N-KB3
12. N-K5!	N(5)-Q4

Prancing the knights around does not necessarily better their positions. Long ago Black should have played B-Q2, leaving his queen knight in place to guard against the incursion of White's king knight.

13. Q-B3	B-Q2
14. Q-R3!	R-B1??

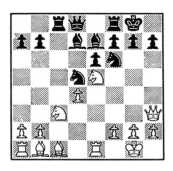

That there are better moves is an understatement. We suggest 14. ... NxN or 14. ... B-B3. Black may answer B-KN5 with P-KN3.

15. NxN!!

Black's king knight is *overloaded.* It must guard against mate on R7 so that the knight's defense of anything else (his colleague on Q4, or the bishop on Q2) is strictly illusory. Black may lose his queen thus: 15. ... PxN 16. NxB! QxN 17. BxP+!! K-R1 18. B-B5+!

185. *Queen's Gambit*

This game may perhaps appear in a future anthology that treats of classic Chess. It was played between Pal Benko and William Lombardy in the 1969 United States Championship, New York City. The game features a subtle trap, the successful culmination of which involves a mini-delayed brilliancy. . . . mini, because it is not necessarily the greatest game ever played; delayed, because after two years, the Turover Brilliancy Prize for the tournament was finally awarded! We present our gem!

The Black "mistake" in this game has often been made before, usually with all the consequences that the loss of a pawn deserves. But here the "mistake" is actually a trap. How surprising that after "winning" the pawn, White loses almost by force.

1. P-QB4	P-QB4
2. N-KB3	N-KB3
3. N-B3	N-B3
4. P-K3	P-K3
5. P-Q4	P-Q4
6. P-QR3	P-QR3
7. PxBP	. . .

White tries to break the symmetry believing his opponent is shooting for a dull draw.

7. . . .	BxP
8. P-QN4	B-R2
9. B-N2	0-0
10. Q-B2	. . .

True the advantage of the first move can allow for one liberty at least without positional deterioration setting in, But White can enjoy a temporary pull after 10. B-K2 P-Q5 11. PxP NxP 12. NxN BxN 13. 0-0 N-K5?! 14. NxN BxB 15. R-R2 B-K4 16. B-B3. Perhaps the Black bishop pair will suffice to keep him out of trouble.

10. . . .	Q-K2
11. B-K2	. . .

Having no desire to open up dangerous lines with 11. PxP, White returns the tempo gained on move eight.

11. . . .	PxP
12. BxP	P-QN4
13. B-Q3	B-N2
14. 0-0!	. . .

There are no complications after 14. N-K4?! NxN 15. BxN QR-B1! 16. BxP+ K-R1 17. Q-N1 (16. . . . N-Q5 was threatened.) P-B4! 18. B-N6 NxP! 19. PxN (19. 0-0 B-K5 20. Q-Q1 KR-Q1 21. N-Q4 Q-N4 22. Q-R5+ QxQ 23. BxQ N-Q6 with advantage to Black.) 19. . . . QxP+ 20. K-B1 Q-N5 21. N-K5 QxP+ 22. K-K2 QxR 23. QxQ BxQ 24. RxB R-B7+ and RxB and wins. Not good after 19. 0-0 is 19. . . . BxN 20. PxB Q-N4+? 21. K-R1 QxB 22. R-N1! and White wins.

| 14. . . . | QR-B1 |
| 15. Q-K2 | . . . |

A tempo must be lost to transfer the queen to a safer square.

| 15. . . . | N-N5! |

The positional threat of N-K4-QB5 puts White on the defensive. Unhappy with such a gloomy prospect White decides to take advantage of the "mistake".

| 16. P-R3?! | . . . |

Better is 16. KR-Q1 or QR-B1.

| 16. . . . | KN-K4! |
| 17. NxN | NxN |

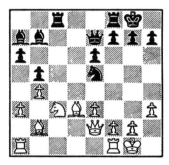

Now White must content himself with 18. N-K4 NxB 19. QxN KR-Q1 20. Q-N1, not very appetizing.

18. BxP+	KxB
19. Q-R5+	K-N1
20. QxN	P-B4!!

Not so obvious since the move allows White free play along the long Black diagonal. Black threatens to win the queen: 21. . . . B-N1 22. Q-Q4 KR-Q1 23. Q-N6 R-Q3 24. Q-R5 B-B2!

| 21. QR-Q1?! | . . . |

Somewhat better is KR-Q1; but then Black is able to enforce P-KB5 with effect. Also possible is 21. Q-N3 R-B5 22. QR-B1

(Or 22. P-B4 P-K4!) P-B5! 23. PxP R(5)xBP 24. R-B2 (Or 24. N-Q1) R(1)-B4 with a fearsome attack.

21. ...   B-N1
22. Q-Q4   ...

Now for the delayed brilliancy. But there are two ways: 22. ... BxNP! and. ...

22. ...   **B-B6!!**

It seems unjust to affix a double exclamation to this move since BxNP has approximately the same effect, besides immediately winning the pawn. The text is prettier though, if only because it is less materialistic. After 23. Q-Q7 Q-N4! 24. QxP+ K-R1 25. P-N3 BxP and mate cannot be avoided.

23. PxB   ...

Here White proposed a draw no doubt envisioning 23. ... KR-Q1 24. Q-N6 Q-N4+ 25. K-R1 Q-R3 26. K-N2 Q-N4+ etc. But. ...

23. ...   **R-B5!!**

Now on 24. Q-Q7 the knockout is 24. ... Q-N4+ 25. K-R1 R-R5 and mates.

24. QxR   PxQ
25. N-K2   R-Q1

Frequently a rook, knight and pawn is enough for a queen, but here Black's queen is too mobile. The conclusion is instructive.

26.	P-B4	K-B2
27.	RxR	QxR
28.	N-Q4	Q-Q4
29.	R-B1	P-N4!
30.	PxP	P-K4!!
31.	N-B2	. . .

A piece also goes after 31. NxBP Q-Q7.

31.	. . .	Q-Q7
32.	N-K1	. . .

Zugzwang results after 32. P-QR4 P-B6 33. B-R3 B-Q3 34. P-R5 K-N3 35. P-R4 K-R4.

32.	. . .	QxB
33.	RxP	Q-R8
34.	K-B1	P-K5
35.	R-B5	B-K4
36.	K-K2	B-B6
37.	N-B2	Q-N7

Rubbing salt into the wound. Everything must go; so White goes too—over the time limit!

186. *Queen's Gambit*

A rook on a file opposes the queen, the queen hastens to effect a pin, but White demonstrates the mobility of a seemingly pinned piece.

1.	P-QB4	P-K3
2.	N-KB3	N-KB3
3.	P-QN3	B-K2
4.	B-N2	0-0
5.	P-K3	P-Q4
6.	P-Q4	P-QN3

7.	B-Q3	B-N2
8.	0-0	QN-Q2

This position in the Queen's Gambit Declined has been reached many times before in master play. Both sides have ample opportunity to be creative.

9.	QN-Q2	P-B4
10.	Q-K2	N-K5

Because his king bishop was rashly developed on K2, Black must lose time to find a safe haven for his queen.

11.	QR-B1	R-B1
12.	KR-Q1	Q-B2?!

Or settle for an unsafe square.

13.	BPxP	KPxP
14.	PxP	PxP
15.	N-Q4!	Q-K4?

Escaping the pin on the queen bishop file, but misapplying the pin on the long diagonal. Better is B-KB3.

16.	N-B6!!	Q-K3

Now White eliminates a vital defensive piece. Of course, 16. . . . QxB loses the *ox* (17. NxB+).

17.	NxB+	QxN
18.	BxN!	PxB
19.	N-B4	B-R3

The *bishops of opposite colors* actually favor the attacker; in other words, this condition rarely guarantees the *draw*. *Warning*: an inexperienced player often is lured into swapping down to an unfavorable *"bishops of opposite"* situation.

20. BxP!!	KxB
21. Q-N4+	K-R1
22. RxN	P-B4
23. QxBP!	RxQ
24. RxQ	BxN
25. RxB	R-Q1
26. P-KN4!	

Opening the royal escape hatch and so ready to harvest the remaining enemy pawns.

187. *Queen's Gambit*

Theory consistently dares White to make something of this mode of defense. Unaware of current theory and practice, Black dares too much. The utmost simplicity nets White the point. Two world championship contenders played this game.

1. P-Q4	P-Q4
2. P-QB4	P-QB4?!

The center should be bolstered by P-QB3, P-K3, or even N-KB3.

3. PxQP!!	N-KB3

Fine so far. Theory discourages 3. ... QxP 4. N-KB3 PxP 5. N-B3 Q-QR4 6. NxP N-KB3 7. N-N3 as favorable to White.

4. P-K4!	...

Black cannot believe his eyes, a central pawn for nothing! But here indeed is the latest wrinkle.

4. ...	NxKP
5. PxP	NxBP

Observe the drawbacks of the following line: 5. ... Q-R4+
6. B-Q2 NxB (6. ... QxP 7. Q-R4+ wins the horse.) 7. NxN
P-K3 (7. ... QxBP 8. R-R1 wins a bishop.) 8. P-QR3 followed
by P-QN4.

6. N-KB3   . . .

Preventing P-K4.

6. ...   **P-K3**
7. N-B3   **PxP??**

How often is the simple development the right way—B-K2!

8. QxP   **Q-K2+**

After 8. ... QxQ 9. NxQ Black's game is in chaos. Unfortunately, even after the text it is no better organized.

9. B-K3   **N-B3**
10. B-N5   **B-Q2**
11. O-O   **N-K3**

Had Black foreseen the future he would have gladly given
a pawn: 11. ... 0-0-0 12. BxN(4) QxB 13. QxP.

12. N-K5!   **NxN**

On 12. ... 0-0-0 13. BxN BxB 14. NxB RxQ 15. NxQ+ etc.

13. QxN   **BxB**
14. NxB   **P-QR3**

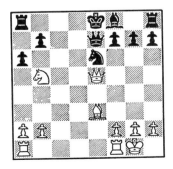

No threat at all. At least P-B3 and K-B2 represents an escape attempt.

15. QR-Q1!	R-Q1
16. B-N6!	RxR
17. RxR	P-B3
18. Q-KB5	P-N3
19. N-B7+	K-B2

Or 19. ... NxN 20. Q-B8+ K-B2 21. R-Q7 winning the queen.

20. Q-Q5

The pin is decisive as R-K1 is coming.

188. *Queen's Gambit*

A similar mating theme is found in a *Two Knights Defense* in this volume. Starting out with central hanging pawns, Black becomes anxious and heads for a premature simplification.

1. P-Q4	P-Q4
2. P-QB4	P-QB4
3. N-KB3	QPxP
4. N-B3	PxP
5. QxP	QxQ?

Correct is 5. ... B-Q2 followed by N-QB3.

| 6. NxQ | P-QR3 |

Preventing N-QN5.

| 7. N-Q5 | K-Q1 |

Or else N-B7+ forking the king and rook.

| 8. B-Q2!! | N-Q2 |

8. . . . . P-QR4 prolongs the game.

9. B-R5+	P-N3
10. N-B6+	K-K1
11. N-B7	Checkmate.

189. *Queen's Gambit Accepted*

The isolated pawn is a weakness, true enough; yet very often it can be the spearhead of a violent attack. In the worst way Black wants to complete his development, a fine idea in itself, but first he ought to have blocked the *isolani*.

1. P-Q4	P-Q4
2. P-QB4	PxP
3. N-KB3	N-KB3
4. P-K3	P-K3
5. BxP	P-B4
6. 0-0	P-QR3
7. P-QR4!	. . .

Favored by Botvinnik in his first match against Petrosjan, the move has merit in that it restricts Black's queen side, demerit in that it leaves QN4 available to Black's pieces.

7. . . .	N-B3
8. Q-K2	B-K2
9. R-Q1	0-0
10. N-B3	Q-B2
11. P-QN3	PxP
12. PxP	. . .

White has set no special problems for Black in the opening. In fact, by devilishly dull play he has half succeeded in anesthetizing the defender. Based on this we must recommend

passive and boring play, that is, if by such tactics an opponent is lulled to sleep. After all, not every game can achieve
the optimum of beauty and excitement.

| 12. ... | N-QN5 |
| 13. B-N2 | B-Q2? |

Selection of one of the following was mandatory: Q-Q1,
R-Q1, P-QN3, or finally N-Q4, which blocks the pawn. Observing his own king bishop undefended, Black should smell
something in the air. As long as the bishop hangs on the same
line as the enemy queen the king pawn will be pinned, and it
is this pin that makes White's thrust so effective.

| 14. P-Q5! | PxP?? |

The derogatory mark is superfluous since there is no saving
clause. But as long as one plays, one must try: QR-K1.

| 15. QxB! | N-B3 |
| 16. NxP | ... |

Here's a curious line: 16. QxN PxQ 17. NxP Q-R4 18. B-B3
Q-Q1 19. NxP+ K-R1 20. NxB+ P-B3 21. NxP RxN 22. RxQ+
RxR 23. BxR mate. The reader should give free reign to his
imagination. But back to our conclusion.

| 16 ... | NxN |
| 17. Q-N5! | |

Black cannot hold the knight on Q4 and defend the mate
at the same time.

190. *Queen's Gambit Accepted*

A *discovered check* is hard to resist, especially if a tasty pawn is the bait.

1. P-Q4	N-KB3
2. P-QB4	P-K3
3. N-KB3	. . .

Evidently White wants to avoid the Nimzo–Indian Defense.

3. . . .	P-B4
4. P-K3	. . .

Neither is the Benoni to his taste.

4. . . .	P-Q4
5. N-B3	QPxP

Let's hope he prefers the Queen's Gambit Accepted!

6. BxP	P-QR3
7. 0-0	P-QN4
8. B-Q3	B-N2
9. Q-K2	QN-Q2
10. R-Q1	Q-B2
11. P-K4	. . .

Better is 11. B-Q2.

11. . . .	PxP
12. NxQP	B-B4
13. N-N3	B-N3
14. B-N5	. . .

Black puts his queen out on a limb to refute White's natural, or rather routine play.

14. . . .	Q-K4!
15. B-R4	0-0
16. B-N3	Q-N4
17. P-K5	N-R4

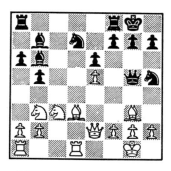

There's nothing like a one-move combination to wrest a pawn from an unsuspecting opponent. 18. B-K4 avoids the trap.

18. BxP+	KxB
19. RxN	NxB
20. PxN	QR-N1!

Confronted by this simple rejoinder, White queried, "You play for a win?" Play Chess!

21. P-KN4	Q-B5
22. QR-Q1	R-KR1!

Acceptance of the bait allows a mating attack along the king rook file.

23. Q-Q2	QxNP
24. Q-B2+	K-N1
25. RxB	. . .

Giving up the exchange avoids mate but the game is lost anyhow.

25. . . .	RxR
26. N-K4	R-N1
27. N(3)-B5	Q-R4
28. N-N3	QxP!
29. N-Q7	QxN
30. NxB	Q-R5

White's material deficit is permanent and therefore fatal.

191. *Queen's Gambit Accepted*

The theme: the overloaded piece. This time it's the king who must look after both his lady the queen and his pawn sitting on the often-explosive KB2. Such a task is aggravated all the more by our sponsor the pawn-grabber.

1. P-Q4	P-Q4
2. P-QB4	PxP
3. N-KB3	N-KB3
4. N-B3	. . .

Not the most solid, but certainly the most trappy and aggressive.

4. . . .	P-B4?!

Correct is P-K3.

5. P-Q5!	P-K3
6. P-K4	PxP
7. P-K5!	. . .

The whole line is one big disastrous trap!

7. . . .	P-Q5?

The only move is N-N5, but Black seems determined to head downhill.

8. BxP!!	B-K3

317

Survival demands N-N5. If 8. . . . PxN, 9. BxP+!

9. BxB!	PxB
10. PxN!	. . .

The eyeopener! 10. . . . PxN 11. P-B7+ wins the queen.

10. . . .	Q-R4

Black relied on this pin to regain his material. Unfortunately, the mating threats White conjures up make the loss permanent. The other possibilities are just as bad: 10. . . . PxN 11. P-B7+ winning the queen, or 10. . . . PxP 11. N-K4.

11. N-K5!	Q-B2

Again the knight is tabu: 11. . . . PxN 12. P-B7+ K-K2 13. B-N5 mate, or 11. . . . PxP encounters Q-R5+.

12. Q-R5+	P-N3
13. Q-N5	PxN
14. P-B7+	. . .

Black's queen is lost.

192. Queen's Gambit Accepted

The recurring theme of the imaginary pin! An aggressive opening once more panics the opposition, either that or Black has delusions of grandeur!

1. P-Q4	P-Q4
2. P-QB4	PxP
3. P-K4	. . .

Employed as a surprise, this move merits consideration, although there is no guarantee of success. The normal 3. N-KB3 is very well analyzed, a good reason for selecting the text.

3. . . .	P-K4

Just as good as P-QB4 but not as sound as P-K3.

4. N-KB3   ...

Not very appetizing is 4. PxP QxQ+ 5. KxQ N-QB3 6. P-B4 B-N5+ and 0-0-0 with a strong initiative for Black.

4. ...	PxP
5. BxP	B-N5+
6. QN-Q2	N-QB3
7. 0-0	N-R3?

There is nothing to fear after 7. ... N-B3 8. P-K5 N-Q4.

| 8. N-N3 | B-N5 |
| 9. B-Q5 | N-K4?? |

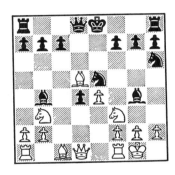

Despite himself, Black can still defend with 9. ... Q-Q2; instead he elects to drive home an imaginary pin.

10. QxP!	NxN+
11. PxN	BxP
12. BxN!	...

A genuine pin for the king rook is loose behind the ranks. If 12. QxB, then Q-Q2, threatening Q-N5 or Q-R6.

| 12. ... | Q-Q2 |
| 13. Q-K5+! | |

White has defended against Q-N5+ or Q-R6 and so he may withdraw his bishop to K3 remaining a knight to the good.

193. *Queen Pawn* (*Modern Colle System*)

The opening bears this name because White's queen bishop, usually undeveloped until the advent of the K4 break, is already effectively developed. White mounts an assault against the castle. Black's desperation is premature as is the concomitant pawn-grab.

1. P-Q4	P-Q4
2. N-KB3	N-KB3
3. B-B4!	P-K3
4. QN-Q2	QN-Q2
5. P-K3	B-K2
6. B-Q3	P-B4
7. P-B3	0-0?!

Better is P-QN3 and B-N2.

8. P-KR4!	P-QN3
9. P-KN4	NxP?

These days they're even bottling water!

10. BxP+	KxB
11. N-N5+	K-N1
12. QxN	N-B3?

Carelessness is a great extravagance in a tight game; ... P-B4 helps close the gaps.

13. Q-K2	P-N3

Helpmate!

14. P-R5!	NxP
15. RxN!	PxR
16. QxP	BxN
17. BxB	P-B3
18. Q-N6+	K-R1
19. 0-0-0	

Black resigns before mate.

194. *Queen Pawn* (*Wing Game*)

The ingredients of a hapless opening: a bishop moved three times, and knights in concert moved no less than nine times!

1. P-QB4	P-QB4
2. N-KB3	N-KB3
3. N-B3	N-B3
4. P-Q4	PxP
5. NxP	P-K3
6. P-KN3	B-B4?!

At one time 6. ... Q-N3 was considered best: 7. N(4)-N5 B-B4 8. P-K3 (8. N-Q6+ K-K2!) P-QR3! with a good game.

7. N-N3	B-N5
8. B-N2	P-Q4?

Displaying chronic symptoms of anxiety. Safer is 8. ... 0-0 9. 0-0 P-QN3 followed by B-N2 neutralizing the enemy king bishop. The text allows his opponent a reduction to a winning ending.

9. PxP	NxP

9. ... PxP, accepting the isolated queen pawn, paradoxically is sounder.

10. P-QR3!	BxN+
11. PxB	0-0

After 11. ... NxP 12. QxQ+ NxQ 13. B-N2 White is much better.

12. P-QB4! . . .

When the queens disappear, Black will fall into a hopeless bind.

12. ...	N-N3
13. QxQ	RxQ
14. P-B5	N-B5
15. N-Q2	N-Q5

Apparently aggressive but factually a waste of time. Better is ... NxN.

16. R-R2! N-R4

Now even 16. ... NxN would not have helped.

17. B-N2	N(4)-B3
18. P-K3	N-B4

... N-B7+ loses the knight: 19. K-Q1!

19. K-K2	B-Q2
20. B-QB3	QR-B1
21. R-QN1	R-B2
22. R(2)-N2	B-B1
23. N-B4	P-QN3

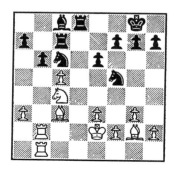

Black must lose a pawn: 23. ... N(3)-K2 24. B-R5(!); 23. ... N(4)-K2 24. N-Q6(!); 23. ... K-B1 24. N-R5 R(1)-Q2 25. NxN PxN 26. B-R5 R-N2 27. BxP and there ain't no more!

24. PxP	PxP
25. NxP	

And the rest is a matter of technique.

195. *Ragosin Defense*

Master and beginner know that the queen is the most powerful piece on the board. Some say, "Capture the queen and victory is assured." Misapplication of such hard and fast rules has caused much sorrow. The Chess player, eager to win the queen, gives no thought to the cost. He gives three, even four pieces. What's even more striking here is that Black gets only a rook and a bishop for the coveted lady. Let's not take the queen lightly!

1. P-Q4	N-KB3
2. P-QB4	P-K3
3. N-QB3	B-N5
4. Q-B2	N-B3

This move characterizes the Ragosin. True the knight blocks the QB pawn but the idea is to open the center with P-K4.

5. N-B3	P-Q4
6. P-QR3	BxN+
7. QxB	N-K5
8. Q-B2	P-K4

The pawn sac frees Black's game. With the lead in development he has the initiative. Yet he must be prepared to play energetically lest White's bishop pair become a permanent asset.

9. QPxP	B-B4

Threatening N-N6.

| 10. Q-R4 | 0-0 |
| 11. B-K3? | . . . |

An attempt to win Black's queen pawn but a serious neglect of development. Better is P-K3.

| 11. . . . | P-Q5! |

One way to catch an opponent is to fall into his imaginary trap.

| 12. R-Q1 | . . . |

12. . . .	PxB!!
13. RxQ	PxP+
14. K-Q1	KRxR+
15. K-B1	P-QR3!!

Najdorf once said that victory is assured after check, check and P-R3!

| 16. Q-N3 | . . . |

Black gets the queen back with a winning position in all variations!

16. . . .	N-B4
17. Q-B3	N-R4
18. P-K4	N(R)-N6+

RESIGNS

The choice: return the queen or get mated.

324

196. *Reti Opening*

The early exchange of queens is no solution. White plays a listless opening and watches the advantage of the first move disappear. Suddenly Black begins an advance in the center. White gets frantic and seeks relief in trading off the ladies. As a result, and to his great surprise, his king, trapped in the middle of the board, undergoes a ferocious mating attack. Even more amazing, the attack is brought off by puny, but much underestimated, minor pieces!

1. P-QB4	N-KB3
2. P-KN3	P-KN3
3. B-N2	B-N2
4. N-QB3	0-0
5. P-Q3	P-B4
6. R-QN1	N-B3
7. P-QR3	P-K3
8. P-K4	. . .

White is procrastinating. He should proceed with his plan of P-QN4.

8. . . .	P-Q4
9. BPxP	. . .

True, Black gets some pressure, but White should accept the pawn anyway: 9. KPxP PxP 10. NxP NxN 11. BxN R-K1+ 12. K-B1.

9. . . .	PxP
10. KN-K2	. . .

Now it's too late to take the pawn: 10. PxP N-Q5 11. B-K3 R-K1, and the threat of B-N5 is too strong.

10. . . .	PxP
11. PxP	QxQ+!!
12. NxQ	R-K1
13. P-B3	P-N3
14. B-Q2	B-QR3!
15. N-B2	QR-Q1

16. R-Q1	N-Q2!!
17. B-QB1	P-B4
18. N-B3	N-Q5!
19. B-N5	...

"I see one move ahead, the best move!" (Capablanca.)

| 19. ... | N-K4!! |
| 20. RxN | ... |

Mate was threatened!

20. ...	PxR
21. N-R2	R-QB1
22. N-QN4	B-N4
23. P-QR4	PxP
24. PxB	PxP
25. 0-0	PxB
26. KxP	R-B4
27. N-K4	N-B2
Resigns.	

197. *Reti Opening*

The efficient elimination of the fianchettoed bishop spells doom for the man behind the imposing pawn center.

| 1. N-KB3 | N-KB3 |
| 2. P-KN3 | P-KN3 |

3. P-N3	B-N2
4. B-QN2	P-Q4
5. P-B4	P-B3
6. B-N2	0-0
7. 0-0	QN-Q2
8. P-Q3	. . .

The game could have transposed into a favorable Dutch Defense for Black: 8. P-Q4 N-K5! 9. N-B3 P-KB4.

| 8. . . . | R-K1 |
| 9. N-B3 | P-QR3?! |

An obvious improvement is 9. ... P-K4 10. PxP PxP 11. N-QN5 Q-N3.

| 10. P-Q4 | PxP |

Now . . . N-K5 is bad: 11. NxN PxN 12. N-N5!—all because Black's rook at K1 would be misplaced in this continuation.

| 11. PxP | N-N3? |

The break P-K4 allows 12. P-Q5 but Black's pieces would be far more active.

12. Q-Q3	B-K3
13. N-Q2	Q-Q2
14. P-K4	QR-Q1
15. P-Q5?	. . .

A beautiful position spoilt by one careless gesture. After 15. P-B5! QxP? 16. QxQ RxQ 17. N(3)-N1! R-QN5 18. B-QB3! White wins!

15. . . .	PxP
16. BPxP	B-R6!
17. Q-K3?	. . .

One move lost the edge, this move loses a pawn, although not very obviously. Correct is 17. KR-Q1.

17. . . .	BxB
18. KxB	N(N)xP!!
19. PxN	NxP
20. NxN	QxN+
21. N-B3	BxB
22. QR-N1	B-B3
23. Q-N6	QxP!
24. QxNP	P-QR4!

And the rook pawn simply queens.

198. *Slav Defense*

If you're the man with the reputation, the champ of the neighborhood, the park, the city, the state—Who knows?— then, more often than not, your opponent will be anxious to swap off those deadly queens. With the right setting you'll be able to land a live one!

1. P-Q4	P-Q4
2. P-QB4	P-QB3
3. N-KB3	N-B3
4. Q-N3	. . .

Unusual, but not bad. Rather than fight fire with fire Black should continue with 4. ... P-KN3. He may then develop his queen bishop at will.

| 4. ... | Q-N3?! |
| 5. N-B3 | QxQ |

Black is all too ready for a draw. Correct is the simple PxP.

| 6. PxQ | B-B4 |
| 7. P-B5! | . . . |

Perhaps Black knows he has fallen into the soup with the hasty exchange of queens. The open queen rook file combined with a pawn attack, hosted by the White queen knight pawns, guarantees the win!

| 7. ... | N-R3 |

Hoping to prevent P-QN4, but. . . .

| 8. P-K4! | NxKP |

Even after 8 . . . PxP the execution continues.

| 9. BxN | PxB |

With Black's pawn structure destroyed the end is inevitable.

10. N-K5!	NxN
11. PxN	B-B7
12. R-R3!	R-B1

13. K-Q2	P-B3
14. KxB!!	PxN
15. PxP	P-K3

It's too late to get the pieces out; the game is over.

16. B-K3	P-KN4
17. RxP	B-N2
18. B-Q4	0-0
19. RxRP	

Materially and strategically Black is busted.

199. *Slav Defense* (*Exchange Variation*)

Opening simplicity is the greatest deception. J. W. Collins, of MCO fame, slipped this one over.

1. P-Q4	P-Q4
2. P-QB4	P-QB3
3. PxP	PxP
4. N-KB3	N-KB3
5. N-B3	N-B3
6. B-B4	B-B4
7. P-K3	P-K3
8. B-QN5	B-QN5

There is a special talent for securing the advantage in a symmetrical position. There is no set routine. If one does not have the talent—most of us poor plodders—then hard work is the only recourse. Black may safely break the symmetry with . . . N-Q2.

| 9. N-K5! | Q-R4! |

If 10. NxN, then QxB!

10. BxN+	PxB
11. 0-0	BxN
12. PxB	QxBP?

After ... Q-R3 13. P-B3 P-R3 14. R-B2 0-0, the game is completely equal.

| 13. Q-R4! | 0-0 |

Black's queen is stuck!

| 14. QR-B1 | Q-N7 |
| 15. RxP | P-QR4 |

Black should retreat the queen while he may.

| 16. KR-B1 | Q-N5 |
| 17. Q-Q1! | ... |

A deceptively simple position. Black looks in vain for a constructive move. It's there: ... P-R3, providing a retreat (KR2) for the bishop. Instead he finds a *peaceful* move.

| 17. ... | K-R1 |

Too peaceful!

18. P-N4!	B-K5
19. P-B3	B-N3
20. NxB+	RPxN
21. B-Q6!	

And Black loses the exchange.

200. *Slav Defense* (*Winawer Counter-Gambit*)

This gambit is of 100 years' vintage. White can maintain a small edge if he is willing to return the pawn—he is not! We witness an entertaining attack, made possible by his rival's anxiety to escape the pin.

1. P-Q4	P-Q4
2. P-QB4	P-QB3
3. N-QB3	P-K4
4. PxKP	...

Also convenient is 4. BPxP BPxP 5. N-B3 P-K5 6. N-K5.

4. ...	P-Q5
5. N-K4	Q-R4+
6. N-Q2	...

Naturally not 6. B-Q2 QxKP!

| 6. ... | N-Q2 |

Now 6. . . . QxKP loses time after 7. KN-B3.

| 7. P-B4? | ... |

"Gimme that," squeaked the prodigy. White should return the pawn with the thrust P-K6, leaving Black with the worse pawn structure.

| 7. ... | N-R3! |

The knight is not to be denied the post K6.

8. P-QN3	N-KB4
9. B-N2	N-B4
10. K-B2?	...

Correct is 10. KN-B3; however, the real damage has already been done on move 7.

| 10. ... | N-K6! |
| 11. Q-B1 | QxN! |

12. QxQ	N-K5+
13. K-K1	NxQ
14. KxN	B-N5+

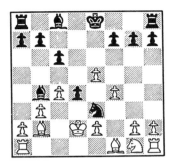

Should the king retreat, his king bishop would be left undefended.

| 15. K-Q3 | B-B4+ |
| 16. KxP | N-B7! |

Three pieces are a mate!

Index To The Traps By Openings

*(Numbers refer to individual variations; numbers in
bold print indicate success for White.)*

KING PAWN

QUEEN PAWN

(Includes, for purposes of indicing, all other openings, such as the Bird, Dutch Defense Reversed, English, King's Indian Reversed, Orangutan, Queen's Fianchetto Opening and Reti, that are not, strictly speaking, characteristically queen pawn.)

OPENING

Some of McKay's Best-Selling Chess Books

- Official Rules of Chess (Second Edition), *by the U.S. Chess Federation*
- Modern Chess Openings, 11th Edition (MCO 11), *by Walter Korn*
- An Illustrated Dictionary of Chess, *ed. by Edward Brace*
- Maxims of Chess, *by John W. Collins*
- Pawn Structure Chess, *by Andrew Soltis* (paperback)
- Chess Fundamentals, *by J. R. Capablanca* (paperback)
- The Game of Chess, *by Dr. Siegbert Tarrasch* (paperback)
- Practical Er.dgame Lessons, *by Edmar Mednis*
- Pawn Power in Chess, *by Hans Kmoch* (paperback)
- Practical Chess Openings, *by Reuben Fine* (paperback)
- The Art of Defense in Chess, *by Andrew Soltis*
- A Short History of Chess, *by Henry Davidson*
- The Art of Sacrifice in Chess, *by Rudolf Spielmann* (paperback)
- My System, *by Aron Nimzovich* (paperback)
- Common Sense in Chess, *by Emanuel Lasker* (paperback)
- The Art of Positional Play, *by Samuel Reshevsky*
- Modern Chess Opening Traps, *by William Lombardy* (paperback)
- The Ideas Behind the Chess Openings, *by Reuben Fine* (paperback) •

For a complete list
of David McKay and Pitman
books on chess, write to:

Director of Sales
David McKay Company, Inc.
750 Third Avenue
New York, N.Y. 10017